Talking About God

The Walter and Mary Tuohy Lectures
John Carroll University

TALKING ABOUT GOD

Doing Theology in the Context of Modern Pluralism

by David Tracy and
John B. Cobb, Jr.

with an introduction by David R. Mason

THE SEABURY PRESS • NEW YORK

1983
The Seabury Press
815 Second Avenue
New York, N.Y. 10017

Printed in the United States of America

Library of Congress Cataloging in Publication Data

Tracy, David.
The problem of God today.

At head of title: The Walter and Mary Tuohy
lectures, John Carroll University.
1. God—Addresses, essays, lectures.
I. Cobb, John B.   II. Title.
BT102.T68   1983   231   82-10293
ISBN 0-8164-2458-6

Contents

Preface

In 1966, Mrs. Mary Tuohy established at John Carroll University the Walter and Mary Tuohy Chair of Interreligious Studies, in memory of her husband, Walter Tuohy, chief executive officer of the Chesapeake and Ohio Railroad. Since then many distinguished scholars have come to the campus to give classes and lectures on topics of interreligious interest. In the 1976–77 academic year, the topic of the Tuohy Chair was "The Problem of God: Resources for Its Resolution," and the Fellows were David Tracy and John B. Cobb. The program was organized by David R. Mason, associate professor of religious studies at John Carroll University. The classes were for our students, but the public lectures were open to all in the greater Cleveland area who chose to attend. The university is pleased to make them available to a wider public.

Joseph F. Kelly, Director
Walter and Mary Tuohy Chair
of Interreligious Studies
John Carroll University

Introduction

The topic for the 1977 Tuohy Chair public lectures, "the problem of God today," is critical for the very lifeblood of any form of theistic faith, whether it be Jewish, Christian, or Muslim. The two scholars who were invited to reflect on the problem with us and to propose "resources for its resolution," John B. Cobb, Jr., and David Tracy, are themselves Christian—the one, Protestant, the other, Roman Catholic. Nevertheless, while each speaks out of his own religious and intellectual tradition and both speak primarily to the Christian community, it quickly becomes apparent that both are sensitive to diverse religious traditions. Moreover, the tentative proposals they advance for treating the problem of God are aimed at any theistic believer who takes seriously the demand to express that faith in a way that is both intelligible and accountable to its initiating religious vision. This book contains the public lectures given by professors Cobb and Tracy in May and June of 1977, as revised for publication.

The initial impression one is likely to gain from an examination of this work is the utterly different way in which each theologian has seen fit to address the issue. Perhaps it should be remarked that the difference is not that between a "Protestant viewpoint" and a "Roman Catholic viewpoint." Anyone conversant with present-day theology knows that it is virtually an open air market. However large a role the particular religious heritage may have formerly played in framing a theologian's ideas, it plays a relatively minor one today. The difference lies, rather, between an approach that views the problem as one of substance and one that views it as one of method.

Cobb, on the one hand, understands "the problem of God today" as a substantive problem arising out of various significant challenges to the traditional Christian doctrine of God as a supreme person

who acts in the world and is chiefly known as the Father of Jesus
Christ. Thus, in accepting the invitation to address the problem of
God and to offer "resources for its resolution," he chooses three
from among the many diverse movements and modes of thought in
the modern world that, in some way, present formidable difficulties
for Christian belief: the scientific worldview, Buddhism, and feminism. And in responding to the challenges each of these presents,
Cobb seeks to reformulate our idea of God in ways that both meet
the challenge and remain faithful to the initial Christian vision of
God.

Tracy, on the other hand, argues that before we can engage in
discussion on such a substantive matter as the doctrine of God, it is
necessary to reflect on the nature of theological language and the
context in which it gets worked out. He sees the problem as deriv-
ing from the diverse religious experiences and the manifold types of
theological language, each of which lays claim to be the normative
Christian way of being and thinking. In response to this, Tracy first
attempts to lay bare the relationship between the different tasks of
theology and the social realities identified with each. He also endeavors to distinguish the different tasks in terms of the modes of
argument, the ethical and religious stances, and the ways of expressing claims to meaning and truth appropriate to each. Then he lifts
into prominence the two classical types of theological language,
analogy and dialectic, analyzes them, and argues that while both
bear witness to important truths, the former, analogy, is better able
to incorporate the insight of the latter than vice versa. Tracy approaches substantive issues regarding the doctrine of God, especially in comparing the major types of analogical God-language in
our day, Thomism and process theology. Even so, his contribution
to the resolution is primarily methodological rather than substantive.

Granting this major difference, it might seem inappropriate to
issue these lectures together as one volume. Yet despite the difference, there are similarities of spirit that join them in a common
undertaking. Some of these are not insignificant, and it is well to
alert the reader to them.

In the first place, both Cobb and Tracy concur that speech about
God today is, in a real sense, problematic. That is, while neither of

them treats the existence of God as problematic, both realize that many of the things that have been said about the nature and agency of God in the Christian theological tradition have been brought into question by much in the modern world. Thus theology's task is not—and cannot be—exclusively dogmatic. That is, theology cannot simply unpack the tradition and attempt to render it acceptable in modern dress. As Tracy says, *all* good theology has an "authentically public character," and that, in part, means that theology must be attentive to the voices in the contemporary, secular world that make claims to express meaning and truth about the ultimate context of our lives. Thus the essentially apologetic task of theology is not a matter merely of working out the strategy for convincing the modern world of the truth of the Christian claims. Theology recognizes meaning and truth in the contemporary situation and this, sometimes, on points that come into conflict with the received tradition. The task of theology is not only to be faithful to its initiating religious experience but to be intelligible in terms that any intelligent, reasonable, and responsible person can understand and evaluate according to accepted public criteria. The second half of this task is what initially raises into prominence the problematic character of some of what the received theological tradition has said about God, but on closer inspection it appears that that tradition may not have been as faithful to the vision of God contained in its original experience as it claimed to be.

Not surprisingly, then, both Cobb and Tracy find resources for the resolution of the God-problem in the very challenges of modernity themselves. Cobb makes this point explicit at the outset and proceeds on that very basis. Each of the three modes of thought and behavior that he examines not only creates a special difficulty for the usual way of conceiving and expressing God, but each contains within it resources for reconceiving God in ways more nearly compatible with what the original witness of faith implies. Feminism, for example, not only radically critiques the specifically masculine imagery of dominance usually associated with divine transcendence, but offers us a vision of wholeness that reforms the notion of transcendence and enables us to grasp anew the meaning of the "kingdom of God" toward which and out of which Jesus calls us to live. Similarly, the other two challenges offer ways of thinking that enable us to conceive God as the source of freedom and the one who is open to all that is, and so the creative and redemptive lover of the universe.

Although Tracy does not formulate the issue in terms of specific challenges to specific doctrines, he finds the challenge in "the wide-ranging character of the symbol-systems and the equally wide-ranging and more elusive nature of the forms of experience and language" which practically constitute Christian theism. In addition, the "crises of meaning," which challenge both traditional Christian formulations and the Enlightenment model of truth, precipitate the effort to clarify the manifold meanings of the "public character" of theology. Tracy's response to the challenge, his ability to interact carefully and creatively with the various dimensions of the contemporary situation, and, above all, his willingness to accept others as conversation partners rather than as adversaries, enables him to work toward a theology that is both faithful to the essence of the Christian tradition and intelligible to any reasonable person today. He tries to illustrate the resourcefulness of interchange by bringing neo-Thomism and process theology together and showing how each can contribute to the other. Moreover, he sees that both of these representatives of the use of analogical God-language benefit from the searching criticism—the "hermeneutics of suspicion"—of dialectical thought.

Finally, the attentive reader will discern an underlying accord between Cobb and Tracy with respect to certain fundamental ways of reconceiving the idea of God. Having said that Tracy's contribution is primarily methodological rather than substantive, it nevertheless remains true that he makes several suggestions that disclose a sympathy with Cobb's avowedly Whiteheadian views. Thus, when he endeavors to bring the modern representatives of Thomism and the advocates of process theology into a fruitful dialogue, he criticizes Hartshorne for failing to understand the historical circumstances in which Aquinas developed his concept of God's real and nominal relations but insists that the neo-Thomists respond to the "crucial Hartshornian question": "Is God really affected by our actions in time and history?" Tracy notes that the Thomists, as well as the Scriptures, assume "that God, as a loving God, is affected," but that they have not worked out a conceptuality that is adequate to this "Christian religious insight." Process thought has. Similarly, Tracy seems clearly to suggest that it is no more "logically coherent to speak of knowing an actual future than of a square circle," a position that process thinkers have advocated for some time. If the future is, by definition, always possibility and never actuality, he says that the neo-Thomists will have to work out more precise and subtle analyses for the perfection terms "omniscience" and "omnipotence." Moreover, Tracy agrees with Hartshorne that the "logic of perfection" entails that "God be unsurpassable by others but not by self" so that in aesthetic matters, if not in ethical matters, God is capable of genuine self-enrichment. Admittedly, Tracy's substantive proposals for revision of God-language are few and often couched in the language of rhetorical question. But, if I have understood them correctly, they are consistent with Cobb's idea of God who, as the source of possibilities, is the ground of our freedom and the one who calls us to transcend our given condition. Likewise, they are consistent with Cobb's idea of God as the one who is "constituted by perfect openness to and reception of whatever is possible as possible and is actual as actual." Finally, it seems to me that Tracy's proposals are consistent with Cobb's realization that the feminist imagery of wholeness is the very corrective needed to free the idea of divine transcendence from its typically male notion of dominance so that we can conceive God purely as "the giver of freedom, who urges us to dare great things, and the assuring lover, who accepts us both in success and failure."

These brief comments pointing to some differences and similarities between Cobb and Tracy can in no way convey the subtlety and richness of their thought. They are written, however, as an invitation to the reader to enter into dialogue with their ideas even as they have with one another and with the ideas of other cultural, philosophical, and religious movements.

David R. Mason
John Carroll University

CHAPTER ONE

The Context:
The Public Character
of Theological Language

by David Tracy

The Public Character of Theology

The specific aim of this section of the book is to articulate a contemporary Christian theological discussion on the doctrine of God. To execute that task in summary form, the logic of the argument will take the following form: The first chapter will articulate the general character of all good theological language as fully public language. The second chapter will argue that the primary theological language for the Christian doctrine of God is analogical language. The third chapter will specify the significant differences and similarities among two major analogical traditions (neo-Thomist and process theologies) and the major contemporary dialectical tradition (neo-orthodox theologies). My hope is that by the conclusion of the third chapter, some appropriate constructive suggestions of my own on this crucial theological discussion of the doctrine of God might make both public and specifically Christian sense.

Each theologian often seems dominated by a single concern. For some that concern takes the form of a particular thematic focus (salvation, reconciliation, liberation) around which cohere all uses of the broad range of the Christian symbol-system and the broad range of experience disclosed by those symbols. For others—myself among them—the wide-ranging character of the symbol-system and the equally wide-ranging and more elusive nature of the forms of expe-

1

rience and language involved in theological discourse occasions the need to reflect first on the character of theological discourse itself before proceeding to more thematic interests such as our present question of the doctrine of God. Moreover, the distinct but related crises of meaning of both Christianity in the modern period and of the Enlightenment model of modernity intensify the need for clarification of the character of any claims to public truth. The related phenomena of historical and hermeneutical consciousness are the chief forces that position the question of the character of theological language at the center of reflective attention for many theologians in our period.

This general and familiar set of questions may take the more specific form of seeking ways to express anew the authentically *public* character of *all* good theology, whether fundamental theology, systematic theology, or practical theology, whether traditional or contemporary, analogical or dialectical. In initially general terms, a public discourse discloses meanings and truths that can in principle transform all human lives in some recognizable personal, social, political, ethical, cultural, or religious manner. For example, Christian theological discourse—here understood as a second-order, reflective discourse upon the originating Christian religious discourse— serves an authentically public function precisely when it renders explicit the public character of the meaning and truth for our actual existence that is embedded in the Christian classic texts.

Before setting forth some more strictly theological implications of that position, however, a few more general comments may clarify the context of this position. When one focuses on the character of theology as an academic discipline one notes certain complexities of the discipline itself. For distinct theologies can be related principally to distinct social realities. Indeed the university setting of theology, by forcing theology to engage itself with other disciplines, also forces to the center of theological attention the public character of any theological statement. This setting, which posits theology as an academic discipline, allows the contemporary academic theologian to reflect upon the social realities involved in doing theology. Since the very choice of the word "public" as a focus logically involves a relationship to social realities (publics), it may prove helpful first from the viewpoint of the sociology of knowledge to reflect on which publics are involved here.

In terms of social realities, fundamental theologies are related *principally* to the social reality expressed but not exhausted in the academy.

Systematic theologies are related *principally* to the social reality expressed but not exhausted in the church, here understood as a community of moral and religious discourse.

Practical theologies are related principally to the social reality of some particular social, political, cultural, or pastoral movement or problematic which is argued to possess major religious import (for example, some particular movement of liberation or some major pastoral or cultural concern).

In terms of modes of argument, fundamental theologies will be concerned principally to provide arguments that all reasonable persons—whether religiously involved or not—can recognize as reasonable. It assumes, therefore, the most usual meaning of public discourse—that is, that discourse available to all persons *in principle* and explicated by appeals to one's experience, intelligence, rationality, and responsibility.

Systematic theologies will show less concern with such obviously public modes of argument but will have as their proper concern the representation, the reinterpretation, the ever-present revelatory and transformative power of the specific religious tradition to which the theologian belongs.

Practical theologies will also show less explicit concern with theory and more with *praxis* as the proper criterion for theology—praxis here understood as practice informed by and informing (often transforming) theory itself in relationship to a particular cultural, political, social, or pastoral need with religious import.

In terms of *ethical* stances, other real differences emerge.

Fundamental theologies will be concerned principally with the ethical stance of honest, critical inquiry proper to their academic setting.

Systematic theologies will be concerned principally with the ethical stance of fidelity to some classic tradition proper to their church relationship.

Practical theologies will be concerned principally with ethical stances of responsible commitment, in praxis situations, to the goals of particular movements and/or groups in addressing particular problems.

In terms of *religious* stances, certain logical differences also emerge.

Both systematic and practical theologians will ordinarily assume personal involvement in and commitment to either a particular religious tradition or a particular praxis-movement bearing religious significance (sometimes—as in James Cone, Rosemary Radford Ruether, and Juan Luis Segundo—to both).

While academic theologians in fact ordinarily share that commitment, in principle they may abstract themselves from religious "faith-commitments" for the legitimate purposes of clarifying the arguments of theological discourse so they may be viewed as public arguments in the obvious sense—argued, reasonable positions open to all intelligent, reasonable, and responsible persons.

Perhaps most crucially, in terms of *expressing claims to meaning and truth,* claims to a genuinely public character, the following differences also seem present and will receive the major attention in section two:

Fundamental theologies will ordinarily be principally concerned to show the adequacy (or inadequacy) of the truth-claims of a particular religious tradition to some articulated paradigm of what constitutes "objective argumentation" in some recognized discipline in the wider academic community.

Systematic theologies will ordinarily assume (or assume earlier arguments for) the truth-bearing nature of some classic religious tradition and thereby provide reinterpretations of that tradition for the present. (In that sense systematic theologies are principally hermeneutical in character).

Practical theologies will ordinarily articulate some radical situation of ethical-religious import (sexism, racism, economic exploitation, environmental crisis, etc.) as the (or a major) situation which the theologian should be committed to transform. In terms of truth-claims, therefore, the transformative praxis implied by personal-communal commitment will be assumed or argued to bear predominance over "theory."

If the situation described above is at all accurate, then it becomes clear that a radical if not chaotic pluralism of paradigms on what constitutes theology as a discipline and the public character of theology is likely to occur. It thereby becomes necessary to study more closely the kinds of arguments that cross the more radical lines of difference and then the kinds of public discussion of the remaining major differences that might profitably occur.

Some Constants and Differences in Theological Discussion: The Need for Reflection on Arguments

Constants:

The route from a chaotic to a responsible academic pluralism within any discipline demands that all conversation-partners agree to certain basic rubrics for an academic discussion. In fact, for theologians such agreement does occur. Central among those already existing rules would seem to be the following:

All theologians agree to the appropriateness (usually the necessity) of appeals to a defended interpretation of a particular religious tradition and a defended interpretation of the contemporary "situation" from which and to which the theologian speaks. Moreover, even within the very general rubrics of this fundamental agreement, two further agreements occur before the major differences surface.

First Constant: Interpretation of a Religious Tradition

In keeping with the demand that a theological position appeal to a religious tradition, all theologians are inevitably involved in interpretation. This in turn implies that some method of interpretation of religious texts and history will be implicitly or explicitly employed and defended. Since the general issues of hermeneutical and historical interpretation can be argued on extra-theological grounds it seems imperative that each theologian clarify her or his general method of interpretation. Included in that clarification should be an explicit argument for any major shift in the rules of interpretation for religious texts or events.

In sum, each theologian should feel obliged to develop explicit "criteria of appropriateness" whereby her or his specific interpretations of the tradition may be critically judged by the wider theological community. For example, consider the present theological discussion between some major forms of "existentialist" interpretations of the New Testament and some major forms of "liberation" (*Exodus*) interpretations of the same document. All or most of the prevailing differences outlined in section one are usually involved in those contrasting interpretations. Still it remains legitimate, even imperative, to bracket all other differences for the moment so that a purely hermeneutical argument can take place on what interpretations the texts can support without further extra-hermeneutical backings or warrants. Once that specific argument is clarified, the conversation-partners may then move on to the equally relevant issue of the present truth-status of the interpreted meanings. If that conversation does not occur, then all the issues at once—and all the differences obscuring this crucial constant—soon emerge to assure that the partners will be talking past one another's theological position.

Second Constant:
Interpretation of the Religious Dimension of the Situation

In keeping with the demand that a theological position appeal to some analysis of the contemporary situation, all theologians are also involved in another constant of theological discussion, that of interpreting or defining the religious dimension of the situation.

This second "constant" is more elusive than the first since some theologians argue for the admissibility of appeals to contemporary "experience" as warrants for a theological statement while others deny this. Yet even before the arguments for and against that position are advanced, an agreement can be reached, I believe, on the following propositions.

Whatever specific interpretation of the phenomenon of religion a theologian follows, she or he assumes or argues for an understanding of religion that, in some manner, involves specific "answers" from specific religious traditions to the fundamental questions of the meaning of human existence. This implies, negatively, a reasoned refusal to employ any strictly reductionist interpretations of reli-

gion—that is, religion is really art or ethics or bad science, etc.,
without remainder. This implies, positively, that although the theologian will often share particular methodological commitments with
her or his colleagues in religious studies, the theologian will also
bear the obligation to raise to explicit consciousness the question of
the truth of, first, an interpretation of the most pressing, fundamental questions in our contemporary situation and, second, the answers provided by a particular religious tradition.

If these premises are accurate, then even before the difficult
question of what constitutes a genuinely public claim to "truth" in
theology is addressed, there is a common assumption on the need
to provide an analysis of the contemporary situation insofar as that
situation expresses a genuinely "religious" question, that is, a fundamental question of the meaning of human existence. A public discussion within the wider theological community is entirely appropriate, therefore, on (1) whether the situation is accurately analyzed
(usually an extra-theological discussion) and (2) why this situation is
said to bear a religious dimension and/or import and thereby merits
or demands a properly theological response.

Although these two sets of questions by no means resolve all the
important differences among models for theology, as a discipline
they do clarify certain crucial constants that cut across theological
boundaries. The second set of questions, moreover, may serve to
indicate when a position in religious studies—whether sociology of
religion, psychology of religion, or philosophy of religion—is also an
implicitly or explicitly theological position.

The Major Differences: What Constitutes a Public
Claim to Truth in Theology

If every theologian does provide both interpretations of a religious tradition and interpretations of the religious dimension of the
contemporary situation, it is also clear that the logic of those interpretations forces the matter of the truth of the questions and answers of the tradition and the questions and answers in the situation
to the forefront of any genuinely theological discussion. Precisely
here, I believe, radical pluralism erupts with a vengeance. Yet to
pose this question to all three disciplines in theology outlined ear-

lier seems entirely appropriate, given the fact that each asserts in some manner the truth of its position. The constant in this second and more complex discussion, therefore, is the articulation of some truth-status to any particular theological position. My wager is that if that articulation can be initially defined, then the significant differences among theological disciplines might surface to allow for a clearer discussion of all claims to truth in the inevitable clashes which ensue, and a university setting is precisely where that discussion is most likely to occur.

Fundamental Theologies

Fundamental theologies share the two constants articulated above. Yet their defining characteristic is a reasoned insistence on employing the approach and methods of some established academic discipline to explicate and adjudicate the truth-claims of the interpreted religious tradition and the contemporary situation. With historical origins in the Logos theologies of Philo and the Christian tradition, these theologies ordinarily possess a strongly apologetic cast, sometimes reformulated as fundamental theologies.

The major discipline usually employed is, of course, philosophy or the philosophical dimension of some other discipline. Philosophy continues to be the discipline especially well-suited for the task of explication and adjudication of such truth-claims as those involved in religious answers to fundamental questions. Granted the pluralism of methods and approaches within philosophy itself, a philosophical discussion will inevitably sharpen this issue of truth. For example, theological claims to truth may be formulated in some version of adequacy to common human experience and/or language or, more elusively, some model of disclosure or even *aletheia*. In any case, an explicitly philosophical analysis of the model employed and its success or failure in application cannot but advance the analysis.

In fundamental theologies, arguments will be formulated in harmony with the rules of argument articulated by a particular philosophical approach. The theologian will employ those arguments first to explicate the truth-claims and then to adjudicate them. The most obvious strength of this position is its ability to explicate and defend in a fully public way all theological statements (indeed its insistence that this be done). More exactly, "public" here refers to the articulation of fundamental questions and answers that any attentive, intelligent, reasonable, and responsible person can understand and judge in keeping with fully public criteria for discourse. The argument for this approach to theology takes some form like the following:

There are inner-theological reasons for this task: that is to say, the character of the fundamental questions that religion addresses and the claims to truth that major religions articulate logically impel a fair-minded, public analysis of those claims.

Hence, even if in fact the theologian is a believer in her or his tradition, in principle as theologian (that is, as one bound by the discipline itself to interpret and reflect critically upon the claims of the tradition and the "situation"), the theologian should argue the case (pro or con) on strictly public grounds

In all such argumentation, personal faith or beliefs may not serve as warrants or support for publicly defended claims to truth. Instead, some form of philosophical argument (usually either implicitly or explicitly metaphysical) will serve as the major warrant and support for all such claims.

These last two factors (understood in the context of the larger, inner-theological argument) clearly distinguish this model of theology from the two remaining models.

Systematic Theologies

The major task of the systematic theologian is the reinterpretation of her or his tradition for the present situation. Since I can find no reasons why anyone holding this position need reject the two "constants" outlined above—interpretation of a religious tradition and interpretation of the religious dimension of the situation—disagreements between this position and the first must take a different form. One form of the argument for systematic theologies can, in fact, be articulated on public, philosophical grounds:

First, the systematic theologian might argue that it is a mistaken judgment to assume that only the model for objective, public argument employed in fundamental theologies can serve as exhaustive of that which functions as genuinely public discourse. Indeed, as

Hans-Georg Gadamer, for example, has argued on strictly philosophical grounds, belonging to a tradition (presuming it is a major
tradition that has produced classics) is unavoidable (given the intrinsic nature—that is, ontological historicity—of our constitution as human selves). Moreover, tradition is in fact enriching, not impover-
ishing (given the radical finitude of any single thinker's reflection
and the accumulation of a wealth of experience, insight, judgment,
taste, and common sense which are the result of acculturation into
a major tradition for anyone willing to be formed by that tradition).

Finally, the Enlightenment "prejudice against prejudices" (as
prejudgments), which is said to inform some earlier models for public truth, disallows crucial human possibilities for meaning and truth.
In art, for example, this prejudice against prejudice disallows an
experience of the disclosure of the truth of the authentic work of art.
In effect, it destroys the truth-disclosure of the work of art by removing the event-character of the work of art and forcing that work
of art to become an object-over-against an autonomous subject who
already possesses exhaustive criteria for "truth" and thereby judges
all artistic truth on "unprejudiced" grounds. On this reading, the
"enlightened" bourgeois critic of the work of art is not superior to
the work. Indeed she or he may be a philistine disallowing a disclosure of any further meaning and truth than that already articulated
in "objective" criteria. The real artistic experience, however, comes
to the one who holds herself or himself open to the potential new-
ness of each work of art; who has made a prior decision that the
experience will prove to be worthwhile; and who thereby *has* pre-
judged each work of art as a potentially enriching experience, one
that can change the person having the experience. In an analogous
fashion, religion, like art, is argued to disclose new resources and
meanings and truths to any one willing to risk allowing that disclosure to happen by faithful attendance to (and thereby involvement
in and interpretation of) that truth-disclosure of genuinely *new* possibilities for human life in a tradition of taste, tact, and genuinely
common (as communal) sense.

With this understanding, the theologian's task must be primarily
hermeneutical. Yet this is not equivalent to being unconcerned with
truth, unless "truth" is exhaustively defined in strictly Enlightenment terms. Rather, the theologian in risking her or his faith in a

particular religious tradition, has the right and responsibility to be "formed" by that tradition and community so that a *communal* taste, a faith-ful tact, a reverential judgment may be expressed through the interpretations of the tradition in new systematic theologies.

Moreover, since every interpretation involves application to the present situation, every theological interpretation will be a *new* interpretation. The criteria for judging its appropriateness and its truth, therefore, will be the general criteria for true interpretation. These criteria include the disclosure (alternatively the *aletheia*) possibilities of new meaning and truth for the situation to which the interpretation is applied.

This argument is dependent upon the assumption that "classics," defined as those texts which form communities of interpretation and are assumed to disclose permanent possibilities of meaning and truth, actually exist. If classics do not exist we may have *tradita* but not authentic tradition as *traditio*. Since even their most skeptical critics grant that the Hebrew and Christian traditions include classical texts, the hermeneutical theologians can argue that they perform a public function analogous to the philosophical interpreter of the classics of philosophy or the literary critic of the classics of our culture.

Any text, event, or person that reaches the level of a classic expression of a particular person, community, or tradition serves an authentically public character. One need not accept the Romantic notions of classic and genius justly criticized by Hans-Georg Gadamer to accept this argument on the ontological truth-status of the classic. Indeed all that need be accepted is the following thesis: A systematic theologian's commitment and fidelity to a particular classical religious tradition should be trusted on two conditions: first, that it reach a proper depth of personal experience in and understanding of (*fides quaerens intellectum*) that very tradition that "carries one along"; second, that appropriate forms of expression (genre, codification, systematic exigency) have been developed to represent that tradition's basic experience and self-understanding in an appropriately academic manner. I will suggest in chapters two and three, moreover, that to develop a systematic theological language for the doctrine of God the systematic theologian should appeal to analogical and dialectical language as the classic and public languages for Christian God-language.

This application to systematic theology of the notion of a classic does involve public criteria: criteria of a depth-dimension of personal experience in understanding a particular classical religious tradition; criteria of proper forms of expression to assure that the first factor does not become merely private or idiosyncratic (as unexpressed). Each of these criteria demands, I realize, far more technical analysis of the notion of a realized experience of some public truth in one's *reception* of a classic along with the notion of the modes of expression (codification, composition, genre, style) in the *production* of a classic before these criteria can be accepted as more than a statement of a thesis.

Since time justifiably does not allow for those technical developments here, allow me to conclude this present argument on the basis of an appeal to intuition (proper only in an initially public appeal). Do we not all properly and publicly assume that those texts, events, and persons that express a particular vision of life with sufficient personal appropriation of the tradition are public documents? Do we not thereby assume that the particularity of a major tradition once personally appropriated does disclose certain public possibilities of personal, communal, and even historical transformation? For example, consider the genuine heroes and heroines of our own blood-drenched century—a Mahatma Gandhi, a Dietrich Bonhoeffer, a Martin Luther King, a Martin Buber, a John XXIII, a Teresa of Calcutta—does not each of these figures show how a deep and committed fidelity to one's own tradition of spirituality discloses universal transformative possibilities for all persons (as Hannah Arendt shows with the example of John XXIII in her brilliant work *Men in Dark Times*)? When any one of us witnesses Eugene O'Neill's *Long Day's Journey into Night*, we are aware that this powerful drama, so personal, indeed autobiographical, to O'Neill, in fact discloses transformative possibilities for all. In short, it has become a modern classic.

All first-rate systematic theology, I believe, serves exactly the same public function as any classical expression. For when studying a Karl Barth, a Karl Rahner, a Rudolf Bultmann, a Paul Tillich, a Martin Buber, one notes in their best systematic works precisely the same kind of reality at work: an experience and understanding of a classic religious tradition united with an intense, intellectual struggle to find proper, second-order genres and modes of reflection to apply that tradition anew (and thereby to interpret it), which frees their work to perform its authentically public character.

In sum, if this brief analysis is accurate, then a case can be made for the public character of the systematic theologian's work as a hermeneutical theologian. "Truth," then, will ordinarily function here as either that disclosure-model or *aletheia*-model implied in all good interpretation. With that working-model for the universality of the hermeneutical task as the true task, precisely a fidelity to and involvement in a classical religious tradition (faith or "belief in") will function as a correct and public theological stance.

Practical Theologies

Practical theologies seem to possess the following characteristics:

1. Like fundamental and systematic theologies they share the two constants described above.
2. They ordinarily argue that some specific form of oppression (for example, racism, sexism, economic exploitation) or some interrelated nexus of economic-social-political-cultural factors (for example, the environmental and energy crises as related to the technocratic system linking and enforcing racism, sexism, and economic exploitation in Western societies) is the major factor in our situation demanding theological response.
3. They either assume or argue that there is a genuinely religious and thereby theological import to the limit-situations impelling their theologies.
4. They ordinarily also argue that a theological response to this situation demands commitment to and involvement in the attempt to remedy the oppressive situation.
5. They usually argue that the major task of theological interpretation should be the reinterpretation of overlooked resources of the tradition which promise hope for a transformation of the situation (for example, "liberation" themes over earlier theologies of liberal reconciliation or existentialist revelation).

In terms of the character of theological truth, therefore, the argument for the greater adequacy of a praxis-model for theology over the two earlier alternatives seems to take two principal forms:

Praxis is ordinarily understood by these theologians as not simply practice but as "authentic" practice (actions in the situation) informed by and informing (sometimes transforming) theory in accord with perceived personal, societal, political, cultural, or religious needs (for example, the need to overcome the perceived inability of even good theological theory to overcome actual alienation). If understood in this way, then the basic argument against the relative inadequacy of all theoretical positions in theology is that theory (including metaphysical theory) cannot sublate praxis but praxis can sublate theory. In one sense, this dictum may prove to be a truism since I am unaware of any major contemporary metaphysical theologian who is strictly intellectualist or rationalist in her or his claims for theory. In a more important sense, however, significant differences on the character of theological truth-claims do in fact emerge.

The first difference is the common insistence among many praxis theologians (especially liberation theologians) that only a personal involvement in and commitment to a specific community or cause struggling for authentic praxis will assure the truth-bearing character of theology (perhaps describable as doing-the-truth).

The second difference follows from the first: a transformationist-model of theological truth as distinct from a disclosure- or correspondence- or adequacy-to-experience-model seems implied by all praxis positions: the claim is that praxis transforms theories just as theory transforms practice into praxis. Theory, in sum, is sublated into praxis; theories of theological truth as either correspondence, adequacy, or disclosure, are sublated into a transformation model whereby the theologian, involved in and committed to transforming a particular praxis situation, may find some truthful way of functioning. The "risk" the theologian takes here is a risk that any human being thus involved must take: the risk that the involvement itself, if authentic, will transform one's ordinary (and possibly alienated) modes of acting and knowing (including one's present models for truth), and thereby free one to develop a "liberation theology" or, alternatively, a "political theology" in a truth-as-praxis-transformative manner. These theologies also seem to assume that the greatest public need in our situation is to liberate ourselves from general or specific forms of alienation or oppression. When they help to do so, these theologies clearly serve a genuinely public function in the full transformative meaning of the word.

This general argument on the sublation possibilities of praxis over theory functions, I believe, as the basic implicit or explicit argument for the greater adequacy of the praxis-transformation-model of theological truth over alternative models.

Conclusion: Pluralism in the Strenuous Mood as a Direction

The major point of this analysis, therefore, is the insistence that once the university setting becomes a central setting for theology, then all three major disciplines in theology do share two constants for discussion and one other constant (namely, the search for a model of theological "truth") which leads to wide and important *but discussable* differences (that is, the meanings of truth for theological statements as coherence, correspondence, adequacy to experience, disclosure, or authentic transformation).

The major differences, to be sure, are so sharp as to encourage an increasing tendency within contemporary theology toward a chaotic pluralism. Yet the differences are also differences on common questions (namely, the character of the fundamental questions of human existence; the proper means to interpret a religious tradition; and the central meanings of any public truth-claims). That fact can and does assure the possibility of a community of genuine public academic conversation wherein (as Plato would remind us) a genuine discussion of the subject matter itself can eventually decide the issues for any authentic participant in real academic conversation.

The possibilities of pluralism "in the strenuous mood" will be enhanced if (more likely when) better arguments for each major position than those presented here are advanced as the discussion continues. One direction for theology to take, therefore, is the self-imposed demand that each theologian be willing to render as explicitly as possible exactly where she or he stands on these three questions and thereby on the nature of the discipline itself. My guess is that if that occurs some substantive differences will prove major and others relatively soluble. On the specific question of the doctrine of

God and appropriate language for that doctrine—namely, analogical and dialectical languages—the remaining two chapters will try to see what some of those real differences are and where the conversation might now move.

CHAPTER TWO

The Analogical
Imagination
in Catholic Theology

by David Tracy

I f the first chapter established the conditions for public discourse
in theology, this second chapter will attempt to advance the
discussion by concentrating upon one little-noticed language in one
major theological tradition, the Roman Catholic. The exercise seems
entirely appropriate since little attention has been devoted to this
question; yet, as I hope to show, only an understanding of what I
here name the analogical imagination can allow one to understand
the God-language employed by Catholic theologians.

There exists an increasingly deliberate attempt among many
Catholic thinkers to explicate the particular vision of reality shared
by Catholic Christians. These latter persons have become increasingly more interested in attempting either to define or at least to
locate some understanding of the common reality shared by Catholic thinkers. As a single contribution to that wider effort, I propose
in this chapter to examine a linguistic feature of Catholic theology
in order to test my hypothesis that a central factor in the Catholic
vision is what I will describe as an analogical imagination. That lan-
guage-game—the various kinds of analogical language expressed by
Catholic theologians—once analyzed, begins to disclose a Catholic
form of life or, alternatively, possible mode-of-being-in-the-world
that bears more investigation than it has thus far received.

It is important to note, however, that my present analysis is con-

17

fined to strictly theological language. I understand that language to be a second-order, reflective language that claims fidelity to the originating religious languages of image, metaphor, symbol, myth, and ritual expressive of the religious sensibility. Although much reflection has recently been devoted to analyzing those originating religious languages—for Catholicism, ordinarily under the general rubrics of the Catholic use of image and ritual or the Catholic sacramental or symbolic understanding of all reality—very little work seems addressed to explicating the form of life disclosed in that properly theological language of analogy, so widely, if not universally, used by Catholic theologians.

The Catholic Model for Theological Reflection: Vatican I Revisited

Analogical language, I shall suggest below, can be found as the predominant language employed by Catholic theologians from Thomas Aquinas to Karl Rahner and Bernard Lonergan. Still, before discussing those more contemporary expressions, it would be well to examine for a moment the too seldom noted model for theology articulated in the First Vatican Council. This curiously overlooked passage in the documents of Vatican I was, in its day, a liberating expression for Catholic theology and is, to this day, the dominant model for theology present, however unconsciously, in the major Catholic systematic theologians. The passage states that theology is the partial, incomplete, analogous but real *understanding* of the mysteries of the Catholic faith. It achieves this understanding in three steps: First, by developing analogies from nature to understand that mystery. Second, by developing—by means of the analogy—interconnections among the principal mysteries of the faith (Christ, Trinity, Grace). And third, by relating this understanding to the final end of humanity.

The key to understanding how liberating this model for theology was in its time is to note that theology is clearly distanced from any attempt at deductive *proof* of mysteries (so favored by the Cartesian scholastics of the day). Instead, after proper tributes to Anselm and Aquinas, theology is described as consisting of analogous but real understanding (*intelligentia*) of those mysteries. Moreover, this pas-

sage is placed in the wider typological context of the document
wherein two alternative types described as rationalism and semira-
tionalism (proofs of the mystery) on the one hand, and fideism and
traditionalism (no analogous understanding) on the other are de-
clared inadequate theological models.

Any historically conscious reader of contemporary Catholic theologians like Karl Rahner, Bernard Lonergan, Edward Schillebeeckx, Johann Baptist Metz, and Hans Küng will note both significant similarities and differences between their theological language
and that of Vatican I. The most significant differences can be found
in the post-nineteenth-century material understandings present in
these theologians of such crucial concepts as "faith" (now as fundamental attitude or orientation; then as cognitive beliefs) or "mysteries" (now usually understood as the radical incomprehensibility of
human existence and divine reality; then as specific and articulated
mysteries). The second significant difference may be described as
the attempt by such theologians as Schillebeeckx, Metz, and Gut-
tierez to incorporate more explicitly dialectical modes of reflection
into the general theological model. And therein lies an important
factor in the contemporary debate on a Catholic theological social
ethic. Sometimes this dialectical turn (as with the Latin Americans)
takes a Marxist form because the social-ethical as analogical view of
society—articulated principally by Jacques Maritain in Europe and
Latin America and by John Courtney Murray in the United States
and expressed institutionally in the Christian Democratic parties of
Latin America and Europe and in the American Catholic commitment (witness Murray) to the American 'civil religion'—have proved,
so the argument runs, inadequate to the present complexities of
contemporary politics, economics, and society. Theologically, however, as far as I can see, these dialectical moves (largely dialectical
negations of oppressive structures) are transformed eventually into
a Catholic analogical context that considerably shifts the final or ultimate envisioned-in-hope reality.

For example, the dialectical methods in the social ethics or, as
the Europeans prefer, the political theology of Johann Baptist Metz
are finally themselves transformed in *Theology of the World* into an
analogical—as sacramental and incarnational—vision of reality constituted by the ordered relationships disclosed in the focal meaning

of the God-human relationship incarnate in Jesus Christ. This cannot but strike an alert reader as worlds apart from the seemingly similar political theology of Jürgen Moltmann. The latter thinker, faithful to his Reformation heritage, sees the dialectical logic of contradiction disclosed in the central symbol of the crucified one as challenging, at its root, all claims to the possibilities of an analogical vision informed by the logic of ordered relationships. Sometimes dialectical methods are employed on less social-ethical and more centrally theological motifs—as in the understandings of justification in Küng, Rahner, and Metz, or the Christologies of Schoonenberg and Schillebeeckx. Although I can only state my conclusion rather than demonstrate it here, the fact seems to be that after those dialectical moments have been employed, an analogical model and its correlative vision reemerge to provide the basic theological horizon of meaning for Catholic theologians. Indeed, I believe that future historians will probably view those present works as an attempted Catholic ecumenical theological incorporation of modern negative dialectical principles into the fundamentally analogical vision of Catholic Christianity.

In sum, the formal model of theological understanding as intrinsically analogous rather than either equivocal or univocal always seems to reemerge in Catholic theologians as the basic linguistic form and thereby the fundamental existential vision of reality informing their work. A historian of Christian theology, I suspect, would find this relatively unsurprising insofar as the common mentor of Vatican I and most Catholic theologians alike, Thomas Aquinas, has ordinarily been interpreted as fundamentally and irretrievably analogical in his vision of reality. Although I agree with this familiar judgment, I have nevertheless become convinced that recent linguistic studies of the logic of metaphor, analogy, and models provide a surer clue to understanding not only Thomas' basic language and vision but that of Catholic Christianity as well. Before trying to spell out the latter factor, however, a brief review of some representative modern interpretations of Thomas on analogy would seem in order.

What, Then, Did Aquinas Mean?
The Thomist Battle Over Analogy

The much-covered, indeed much-littered, terrain of contemporary Thomist interpretations of analogical language on theology cannot be adequately covered short of a full-length book. For the moment, however, I hope you will bear with me as I present my own heuristic device for understanding some of the representative moments in that twentieth-century Thomist self-discovery. That heuristic device will take the form of suggesting that there are five principal schools in the development of modern Thomist understandings of analogy, the fifth or linguistically formulated of which is the most important for the present concern with languages and forms of life.

The schools can be named as follows: first, the modern defenders of the Commentators; second, existential Thomism; third, participation Thomism; fourth, transcendental Thomism; fifth, linguistic analyses of Thomism. In the first group, the prevailing interpretation held that Thomas possessed a single and metaphysical 'doctrine of analogy' that was fundamentally a doctrine of proper proportionality between creatures and Creator. The principal interpreter here, is, of course, Thomas de Vio Cardinal Cajetan whose 'single doctrine' theory, mediated through John of St. Thomas, finds contemporary metaphysical expression in Reginald Garrigou-Lagrange and Jacques Maritain and contemporary logical defense in Bochenski and James Ross. The difficulties with this position—a position of both logical and metaphysical sophistication—are several. Chief among them is the fact that textual analysis (here Klubertanz is the central figure) has argued that Thomas never possessed a single doctrine of analogy but employed several uses of analogical language. Moreover, a systematically essentialist position in the Commentators—and thereby in Garrigou-Lagrange—has been condemned on both historical and philosophical grounds by all four other contemporary schools as radically un-Thomist.

Indeed, the central insistence of both the second and third major schools of modern Thomism—the so-called existential Thomism of Étienne Gilson and the Anglican theologian Eric Mascall and the participation Thomism of Fabro and Geiger and others—have united, in spite of their otherwise prevailing intensive and important differences, to insist that Thomas' own metaphysical position withdrew from the essentialism of Aristotle (wherein form finally dominates act) to articulate a metaphysics where *esse*, or the act of existing, is the central key. Consider the theological formulation of this claim in Eric Mascall. For Mascall, following Gilson, this is the case because Thomas as a theologian (or, alternatively, as a "Christian philosopher") was informed by the biblical vision of God as He Who Is—as Creator and sustainer of all reality, origin and end of all things. This biblical vision transformed all of Thomas' more explicit philosophical commitments. The proper understanding of analogy, therefore, must give (as in Mascall) a central place to an analogy of attribution wherein the *esse* of any creature participates in the pure *Esse* of the Creator in such manner that this metaphysical and theological position informs *any* analogy of "proper proportionality" between God and creatures. Indeed the latter is sometimes formulated by Mascall as the proportionality based on a distinction between essence and existence in creatures and the absence of such distinction in God (for God—and God alone—is The one whose very essence *is* to be—*Ipsum Esse Subsistens*). Therefore, in its clearest theological expression, the work of Eric Mascall, the theological claim is precisely that a metaphysics of *esse*, itself informed by the biblical view of God as Creator, allows for the development of both an analogy of attribution securing divine immanence and an analogy of proportionality securing divine transcendence.

Two other modern philosophical movements emerged within the Thomist circle to rearticulate this latter, more traditionally formulated, metaphysical analogical vision. Cryptically stated, those two movements may be called the incorporation of the modern turn to the subject and then the linguistic turn within Thomism itself.

More exactly stated, the fourth—and now dominant—school of Thomism in theology has come to be called transcendental Thomism and is most familiar to modern readers in the work of Karl Rahner and Bernard Lonergan. What interests me here, however, is not to engage in yet another exposition of Rahner and Lonergan, but to note what happens to analogical language once the transcendental question moves to the forefront of the discussion. The clearest expression of what happens, in fact, may be found in the work of Karl Rahner, more specifically in the too seldom noted change of vocabulary from the first to the second edition of his foundational work in the philosophy of religion and theology, *Hearers of the Word*. In the first edition, one finds the more familiar Thomist vocabulary, "the analogy of being"; in the second edition, the vocabulary shifts to "the analogy of having being." That shift, I believe, is of central importance for understanding Rahner and his extraordinary influence on contemporary Catholic theology. Summarily stated, the shift has the following form and significance: the analogy of attribution now takes the form of having as the prime analogate (or focal meaning) the conscious experience of the knowing, willing, and historically incarnate subject. The analogate is no longer *any* finite being (as with Mascall) but only that being-human being—who is conscious of its being as a *spirit*-in-the-world, always already in the presence (through its conscious as dynamic intentionality) of Pure Being.

The focal meaning for all analogical usage thereby becomes human subjectivity in relation to God as Absolute Being—and theologically as Absolute Mystery. The key to all proper theological usage thereby becomes an explicitly transcendental analogical language developed first in a transcendental philosophy ("analogy of having being" language) and then applied—analogously—to a transcendental theology ("analogy of faith" language). If my interpretation is correct, then it bears noting that however much Rahner may have incorporated either Kantian transcendental, Hegelian dialectical, or Heideggerian ontological modes of inquiry into his own theology, Rahner's entire theology (as Lonergan's) remains profoundly analogical in its fundamental vision of reality.

The theologies of Rahner and Lonergan can be interpreted by their neo-transcendental formulation of the traditional Catholic analogical vision. In this Rahner and Lonergan emerge as splendid modern Catholic mediating theologians of our day whose work, like their Protestant counterparts Bultmann, Barth, Tillich, and the Niebuhrs, must be taken into account by every serious contemporary Christian theologian. Indeed, their transcendental version of the Catholic analogical vision of all reality, I continue to believe, remains an authentically modern and Catholic resource for understanding both the uniqueness of the fundamental Catholic modern, productive imagination as an analogical one and for deciphering the peculiar logic of Catholic theological—as analogical—language. Moreover, the explicitly linguistic interpretations of Rahner and Lonergan in recent years by Victor Preller and David Burrell approach those languages and that vision in a manner which, although in my judgment flawed in a final moment, is genuinely suggestive of a way of understanding theological language for all students interested in the analyses of theological languages as disclosive of a particular form of life or a specific vision or imagination of the whole.

I cannot hope to do justice to Burrell's important linguistic studies of Aquinas' analogical language in these brief remarks. Suffice it to say, therefore, that the explicitly linguistic approaches Burrell has espoused (to a chorus of disdain from many Thomists and an echoing silence from other theologians) are an excellent modern linguistic key to the questions of analogical usage. Indeed, since I share Burrell's judgment that the interpretive works of Rahner and Lonergan on Aquinas are the central *contemporary* Catholic theological texts needing explicitly linguistic analysis, my own position is not as distant from his as either one of ours is from the more familiar analyses expressed by proponents of the first three schools.

Summarily stated, Burrell argues that the key to analogical language in Aquinas can be found in the category "focal meaning." Employing G. E. Owen's interpretation of Aristotle's own insistence on focal meaning in analogy, Burrell argues at considerable textual and historical length that Aquinas in fact employs several specific forms of analogy. Yet central to all those uses for Aquinas is an understanding on the part of the authentic and reflective inquirer (in Lonergan's Thomas interpretation)—now reformulated by Burrell as the good language user—that the focal meaning character of analogical language must be proportionally extended to all other analogous usages. The influence of Lonergan's form of transcendental Thomism here is obvious and, although admittedly arguable, is, I believe, fundamentally sound. What is novel is the insistence that the logic of analogy bears striking resemblances to the more familiar logic of metaphor.

Since this same insistence is the major burden of my own constructive remarks, I will now depart from these brief and more contextual comments in order to concentrate upon the constructive proposal which I will advance for your critical attention: that the

recent and more familiar studies of the logic of metaphorical usage
in religious language parallel the linguistic studies of the logic of
analogical usage in properly theological language. Correlatively, a
linguistic analysis of that logic discloses an analogical vision of reality
as that religious mode-of-being-in-the-world which is distinctively
Catholic I hope that the more historical and hermeneutical approaches of these first two sections may serve to show that my own
constructive position here on Catholic Christianity is more than an
idiosyncratic one. At any rate, if these analyses of the first two sections have been at all cogent, then the constructive alternative of
my third and final section may be stated in properly summary terms.

Metaphor, Analogy, and the Catholic Imagination

Three widely shared conclusions from recent linguistic studies of
the character and logic of metaphor bear striking parallels to the less
widely known results of linguistic studies of analogy. The first conclusion is a negative one: the assumption that metaphors are merely
rhetorical and decorative substitutions for the true-as-literal meaning has been effectively challenged by recent linguistic study. On
the question of the logic of the Kingdom of God language in the
New Testament parables, for example, the implications of this negation have called into serious question former allegorical and moral
interpretations of these central Christian language forms for many
among the present generation of New Testament scholars.

The second conclusion is more positive: whatever theory of the
logic of metaphor is employed by its various proponents, the crucial
factor to note is that a meaning (not expressible without loss in literal terms) emerges from the interaction of words not ordinarily—
that is, in terms of their literal meanings—used conjunctively. Good
metaphorical usage, as Aristotle long since observed, cannot be
learned by the rules: the capacity to recognize similarity in dissimilarity is a mark of poetic genius. As new emergent meanings explode
in a culture's consciousness, the older and spent ones become merely
dead metaphors and thereby enter our dictionaries.

The third conclusion is, from the viewpoint of theological language, the most important. Since I have tried to defend this contro-
versial conclusion at length elsewhere, I trust you will bear with me

if I simply state it here. The conclusion can be variously formulated: in its more familiar form in linguistic philosophy of religion, one may recall Ian Ramsey's lifelong attempt to show what he nicely called the 'odd logic' of religious language; in its less familiar, but for my part, more adequate formulation, one may cite the recently developed theory of Paul Ricoeur that the specificity of religious language lies in its character as a limit-language, or, alternatively, if I may presume to cite it, one may note my own development of Ricoeur's position to suggest that a careful attention to the "limit-to" character of the language of both limit-situations and limit-questions of our ordinary experience and discourse and the "limit-of" intensified character of explicitly religious language disclose a defining characteristic of the religious use of any language form. That characteristic is its limit-character wherein, by stating a limit-to the ordinary situation one also shows and partly states a language expressing some limit-of, that is, some vision of the whole of reality (God-cosmos-humanity). In relationship to the religious use of metaphor, this linguistic analysis may be viewed in recent New Testament exegeses of the limit-use of the metaphors in parables to disclose distinct religious visions or modes of being-in-the-world in the New Testament itself.

I have summarized this more familiar discussion on the religious language use of metaphor in order to suggest that an exactly parallel analysis is available for the more properly conceptual and reflective language of theology. More specifically, that parallel can be found in the properly analogical language of the Catholic theological tradition.

Indeed that parallel, I have come to believe, applies to each step of the analysis of metaphor. In the first place, the same kind of negative move is made by recent linguistic studies of Aristotelian and Thomist uses of analogical language. For the most important criticism of the Commentator tradition (whether articulated metaphysically, epistemologically, or here, linguistically) is that the great Commentators (Cajetan, John of St. Thomas, and others) failed to understand Aquinas' own highly pluralistic usages of analogical language in their scholastic attempt to systematize a single Thomist doctrine of analogy. That latter and almost canonical doctrine sometimes ended, ironically, in disclosing some form of Scotist univocal language (the language of common being) to bolster the elusive analogical language of Thomas himself. Just as metaphors were once considered mere substitutions for literal meanings, so analogies— now implicitly rather than explicitly—were considered by their major exponents in modern theology to be finally substitutions for the real—the univocal—meaning.

The second and more positive point of these recent linguistic studies of analogical language parallels, once again, the "emergent meaning through interaction" theory of metaphor. For good analogies, like good metaphors, depend on the capacity to recognize what Aristotle called similarity in dissimilarity. This native capacity allows us to break out of accustomed and deceptively univocal usage to describe either the unfamiliar or a forgotten dimension of the familiar. More specifically, analogical usage in both Aristotle and Aquinas is fundamentally a matter of good usage of focal meanings proportionally employed for extended and discriminating meanings—at *the limit, to the whole of reality.* The most important focal meanings, moreover, may be found both in that evaluative language in ordinary discourse used to disclose our purposive projects and in that context-variant language (is, true, good, beautiful) used in ordinary discourse in a manner oblivious of the usual categorical distinctions (namely, the language of the transcendentals—one, good, true) to make cross-categorical or interlinguistic sense of our actual ordinary usage. In sum, the emergent meanings of our analogous terms are not substitutions for a real—a univocal—meaning. Rather analogous terms are good language usage which—precisely as analogous—relate all other usages to the focal meaning of a purposive subject: in Christian language usage, to a purposive subject only in relationship to a God of purpose and action

The third parallel is likewise relevant. For the final clue to the proper use of analogical language in Catholic theology may be found in the use, starting with Aquinas, of perfection terms. The logic of perfection, as Aquinas knew as well as Hartshorne, is an odd, even a limit-logic—indeed, for him, a metaphysical logic—involved in the logical differences among all, some, or none. The dispute between process theologians and Thomists is not primarily, on this reading, a dispute between one group that understands the peculiar logic of perfection terms and one that does not. Indeed, the dispute is usually not even focused upon whether analogical language is the appropriate language for God-talk as perfection-talk. Finally, as the process commitment to the paradigm of human experience expressed in the reformed subjectivist principle of Whitehead shows, the dispute between transcendental Thomists and process thinkers is not even over the choice of *the* primary focal meaning for all analogical God-talk as the subject: experiencing, inquiring, reflecting, and purposive in relationship to God. Rather, on this reading, the central dispute between these two major contemporary theological expressions of the analogical language of perfection-terms as the key to proper God-language is fundamentally a dispute not over the odd or limit-logic of perfection or over the intrinsically analogical-as-focal-meaning character of such language. The heart of the dispute is focused on the philosophical and religious anthropology operative in the different understandings of what constitutes those *human* aspirations providing the focal meaning for the perfection-language analogously employed for God-language.

In either of these two major theological traditions of our day which employ analogy as their primary language (the Catholic incarnational and the American process traditions), therefore, a vision of the whole of reality is disclosed that is intrinsically analogical; a vision of proper speech for God-language, for example, is articulated which ends in declarations—as in Karl Rahner or, in more muted tones, in Schubert Ogden—of the disclosure of the radical mystery and intrinsic incomprehensibility of the God religiously encountered in faith. Yet the route to this declaration is a familiar Catholic theological route: a route which insists that reason can be trusted to bring one to this point of disclosure of mystery; that reflective language—if properly analogical language—can be trusted to lead the good language-user to that self-discovery; that this theological language—precisely as faithful to the limit-logic of perfection-terms—becomes properly metaphysical language; and, finally, that this analogical language of reflective theology is hermeneutically faithful to the logic and thereby the experience and insights of the originating biblical religious language of metaphor, parable, narrative, symbol, and myth.

CHAPTER THREE

Analogy and Dialectic: God-Language

by David Tracy

The first two chapters argued for the public status of analogical and dialectical languages as the classical theological languages for speech about God. The present chapter will attempt to illustrate those languages more systematically by summary analyses of representative contemporary languages in the present pluralist situation. The chapter will have two main sections: a first section will continue the analysis of some significant differences and similarities between the two major representatives of analogical language for God: the neo-Thomist and the process traditions. The second section will analyze the development of analogical languages within Protestant neo-orthodoxy wherein the starting point is one of negative dialectics. A final, brief section will attempt to comment on where the substantive conversation might proceed from this point forward.

Analogical Languages for God: Neo-Thomism and Process

In the last chapter I attempted to sort out the five major types of neo-Thomism in the modern period of theology. For myself, the most serious candidates for an adequate public contemporary position on analogical language remain the last two forms of Thomism. For the peculiarity of both the transcendental Thomists and their linguistic successors is precisely that Marechal, Coreth, Rahner, Lonergan, Preller, and Burrell insist upon the need to take that turn to the subject distinctive of modernity before proceeding to develop adequate metaphysical and theological languages for the doctrine of God. This factor alone allows for the development of a substantive conversation with the process tradition whose own point of departure for metaphysics and theology is human experience, most appropriately expressed in Whitehead's reformed subjectivist principle.

If one grants the remarkable coincidence of a similar point of departure (human experience) and a similar language and imagination (analogy), it seems curious that the conversation to date between transcendental Thomism and process thought has been, with a few notable exceptions, frustrating to both sides.

The major reason for this frustration, I suggest, is that neither the real similarities nor the real differences between these two traditions have been analyzed with sufficient precision. The similarities have already been stated but are worth noting again: a similar point of departure for analysis (namely, human experience); a similar insistence on the need for metaphysical language directly related to that point of departure; a similar explicit employment of analogical language and thereby the implicit use of an analogical imagination for God-language.

The differences are, in fact, less easy to locate with technical precision. In one sense, of course, the major difference is obvious and all-important. For since Charles Hartshorne's magisterial, lifelong effort to explicate a di-polar conceptuality for God it is obvious that process panentheism and Thomist classical theism are logically, metaphysically, and theologically distinct positions.

Yet the discussion of the real differences has not been aided, I fear, by certain crucial misinterpretations of the opposite position by the conversation partners. When Charles Hartshorne, for example, performs a fundamentally ahistorical interpretation of Thomas Aquinas' exact position on real and nominal relations between God and world, he assumes that Aquinas is responding to our contemporary question of whether God is really affected by our actions. In fact, Thomas is responding to a quite distinct question.

When a distinguished neo-Thomist like David Burrell correctly criticizes Hartshorne's hermeneutical error here, he does not follow that observation with a real neo-Thomist response to the crucial Hartshornian question, that is, is God really affected by our actions in time and history? On religious grounds, Burrell, with the Scriptures (and with Thomas and with the process tradition), assumes that God, as a loving God, is affected. On theological grounds, neither Thomas nor Lonergan nor Rahner nor Burrell, as far as I can see, develops new Thomist conceptualities for God-language in fidelity to that Christian religious insight. In this confusing situation, we seem left with something like armies clashing in the night whereby unguided missiles are hurled by each side (the charge of anthropomorphism to process thought; the charge that Thomas' God is Aristotle's "Unmoved Mover" to the Thomists) and a genuine conversation seems unlikely to occur.

The first significant question that each side should address on its own grounds, I suggest, is a purely logical one: namely, can we coherently conceive of the concept "future" in terms of actuality rather than possibility? If we cannot, then Hartshorne's major point must be accepted on purely logical grounds. The neo-Thomists, in turn, should be invited to develop, on their own philosophical and theological principles, a genuinely Thomist but genuinely new (neo-Thomist) set of concepts for God's real relation to the world by spelling out the exact meaning of "all-knowing" and "all-powerful" if the future, by definition, is always a possibility, never an actuality. Karl Rahner, in his more explicit systematic christological and Trinitarian reflections, seems to be developing systematic concepts in that direction yet also seems unwilling to make the same philosophical move in relationship to the concept of the nature of God.

If one grants, as Rahner does, that panentheism is not synonymous with pantheism and if one grants further, as I do, that Hartshorne's interpretations of Thomas on real and nominal relations are hermeneutical misinterpretations, then the context seems set for a new conversation on the central issues at stake. First, is God really affected by our actions as the Scriptures and Christian religious practice seem clearly to state? If God is, then do we not need dipolar conceptualities to express this religious insight? Second, is it any more logically coherent to speak of knowing an actual future than of a square circle? If it is not, then do we not have to develop more accurate analyses than Thomas provides for the crucial perfection-terms for God, "all-knowing" and "all-powerful"? I repeat that these questions, the first religious and the second purely logical, do not demand that the neo-Thomists abandon their own metaphysical and theological principles in order to respond to the dilemmas posed by Thomas' formulation. Yet they do demand that those principles be employed to rethink and perhaps retrieve the Thomist heritage in a manner faithful to the religious and logical issues at stake.

If these questions could be reopened between these two major analogical traditions in something like the manner suggested above, then a further line of real conversation could be initiated. If the argument of the last chapter on the focal-meaning character of all properly analogical language is accepted, then a new and genuinely promising line of discussion is available to all participants. It is important to recall that, at least on the basis of my analysis, both neo-Thomists and process thinkers share three crucial assumptions for articulating God-language: First, the character of all good analogical language consists in working out a set of ordered relationships between God, world, and humanity on the basis of some paradigm of human experience chosen as a focal meaning for understanding the character of the whole of reality. Second, if we are to speak intelligible God-language at all, then we must find some analogical way to speak perfection-language. In short, both Thomas and Hartshorne are admirable craftsmen of a language about God that is faithful to the peculiar logic of perfection-terms. Third, a major question for any speaker of analogical God-language as perfection-language becomes, therefore, the question: what are the best candidates for the original focal meanings? Exactly here, I suggest, is where each tradition could learn much from the other and initiate important new developments of its own principles.

The fact is that both traditions employ anthropological candidates for the perfection-language to speak analogously about God. In the neo-Thomist tradition, for example, the sophisticated use of linguistic philosophy to analyze Thomist God-language has allowed us to see that the chief candidates for perfection-terms are those terms that embody human aspirations (appraisal terms—good, just, holy, wise) as well as terms that cross categorical boundaries (the transcendentals—the true and the good).

A similar linguistic analysis of Hartshorne's candidates for perfection-terms, I suggest, would lead to the following conclusion: like the neo-Thomists, Hartshorne chooses as his chief candidates for perfection-language those terms expressive of human aspiration and desire. Unlike the Thomists, Hartshorne introduces a distinction between appraisal-terms. Some appraisal-terms (named by Hartshorne ethical perfection-terms) are exactly the same candidates as Thomas chooses (namely, good, just, holy, wise, etc.). These terms, when applied to God, should be employed exactly as Aquinas employed them. The terms good, just, holy, powerful, wise do allow for an *absolute* maximal case and thereby apply to God's essence as all-good, all-just, all-powerful, all-wise. In sum, the logic of perfection-language not only allows but demands that to speak coherently about the perfect one, we must call God, as the absolute maximal embodiment of all perfections, all-good, all-just, all-powerful and all-wise. On this issue the two traditions join.

Yet Hartshorne in fact proposes another set of candidates for perfection-terms; these candidates Hartshorne names aesthetic perfection-terms. These candidates (sociability, temporality, creative change, enjoyment of beauty, etc.) are also—and this point is easily missed—initially anthropological terms embodying human values and aspirations and, therefore, ought not to be ruled out of court as inappropriate candidates. Unlike ethical terms, however, aesthetic terms (for example, a maximal case of enjoyment of beauty) do not admit an absolute maximal case. This is the case because every new event of beauty would add to what was already enjoyed and the possibilities for variety, harmony, enrichment are thereby infinite.

Yet just because there is no absolute maximal case in these instances does not mean that such aesthetic terms are not candidates for perfection-language for God. For the logic of perfection does demand that God be unsurpassible by others but not by self, and thereby, in these aesthetic matters, capable of genuine self-enrichment. This distinction (overlooked, to my knowledge, in the neo-Thomist tradition) between unsurpassibility by others but not necessarily by self as involved in the concept of perfection is the crucial insight needed. For this appropriate logical move frees Hartshorne to agree fully with Thomas on perfection-language from ethical perfection-terms while adding concrete, aesthetic candidates for perfection-language about God without violating the divine transcendence articulated in the logic of perfection shared by both conversation partners.

If this analysis of the situation is accurate then a serious conversation between these two major analogical God-language traditions can be reopened, freed of polemics and on fully public terms that each party, in principle, can accept. Further discussion by both schools on the rubrics under which any anthropological term embodying human aspiration can serve as an appropriate or inappropriate candidate for a focal meaning for analogical God-language is precisely where the future discussion should move. If that occurs each tradition, in my judgment, will benefit. The neo-Thomist tradition will benefit by recognizing a possibility that it can accept without abandoning its own first principles or even its own metaphysics; in short, a genuine development of Thomas' own position is possible here on Thomist terms. The process tradition will benefit by becoming more aware of the properly analogical character of its God-language and thereby more concerned to articulate the more exact relationships between its somewhat inchoate distinction between the ethical and the aesthetic when the real discussion and the real need is to formulate with greater accuracy a fuller process anthropology. In the meantime, the alternative dialectical tradition on God-language may profitably enter this same discussion with its own resources.

From Dialectics to Analogy: Neo-Orthodoxy

Protestant neo-orthodox theologies comprise a spectrum of diverse and original proposals for theological language in general and God-language in particular. The most obvious linguistic feature of these positions has been their dialectical character. Although I cannot hope in this brief space to provide full analyses of the particularities of each position for a spectrum running from Kierkegaard to Moltmann, it will be profitable, I believe, to note the constancy of a theme of negative dialectics that operates in each and all of these positions.

To recall a central distinction: from a linguistic and logical viewpoint, negative dialectics involves a logic of contradiction that negates illusions, pretensions, and wishful thinking. In its secular form it consists of those major hermeneutics of suspicion about the illusions and pretensions of the claim of a rational Enlightenment consciousness to be able to understand and order the nature of reality through conscious rationality. This moment of negative dialectics can be seen when a Sigmund Freud unmasks the illusion of conscious rationality's self-control by analyzing the all-pervasive reality of the unconscious; when a Karl Marx exposes the illusion of the autonomy of the rational bourgeois thinker by explaining the economic conditions allowing, even enforcing, a prized and illusionary autonomy; when a Friedrich Nietzsche exposes the frenzied will-to-power driving the genteel and urbane value-system of the Enlightenment thinker.

In its theological form, the classic task of Protestant neo-orthodoxy is to expose the possible illusions of all liberal theologies through negative dialectics. In its most familiar forms, the neo-orthodox theologian first employs a retrieved and more realistic Christian doctrine of radical sinfulness to expose the self-deluding character of liberal theological belief in progress and pure, autonomous rationality. In a similar dialectical move, the neo-orthodox theologian casts a hermeneutics of suspicion upon all philosophical analogical languages for God-language by insisting upon the radically transcendent character of God and the infinitely qualitative distinction between God and humanity. For Søren Kierkegaard, the major inspirer of this Christian theological form of negative dialectics and suspicion, analogical God-language, in effect, can only recognize the problem of finitude and thereby work out ordered relationships between God and humanity. In short, at best, analogical God-language transcends the limitations of the aesthetic and the ethical stages of existence and reaches the genuinely religious—but pagan, not Christian—insights of "religiousness a." It cannot face the radical sin and guilt in the heart of every human being; it will not face the infinitely qualitative distinction between God and that sinful human being; it withdraws into ever more desperate attempts to ignore the absolute paradox of the God become man by building intellectual analogies from finitude to the infinite that are less and less successful in masking the emptiness at the heart of its tragic and comic dilemma.

This profoundly Christian negative dialectic, most clearly seen in

Kierkegaard, is precisely what provides the real key—the crucial constant—to the genuinely dialectical moment, the hermeneutics of suspicion, in all forms of neo-orthodox theology.

On this view, the shattering impact of Karl Barth's *Romans*, that "bombshell in the playground of the theologians," is the impact of a profoundly Kierkegaardian negative dialectics exploding upon all analogical visions of God-language with the demand, "Let God be God!" The articulation of the Protestant principle by Paul Tillich remains his major and consistently employed principle of negative dialectics from his earliest formulations through his method of correlation, his lifelong attempt to reunite the radically separated human being with the transcendent and reuniting God. The Christian theological drive behind Rudolf Bultmann's program of radical demythologizing is not, as many still think, his desire to render Christianity meaningful to modernity but his insistence that the Christian gospel itself involves a negative dialectic upon all human achievement and pretension including the mythological expressions of the Scriptures themselves. When Jürgen Moltmann, faithful to this neo-orthodox program of negative dialectic, casts doubt upon any analogical language to speak rather of the Crucified God he reexpresses the central insight of negative dialectics for the contemporary setting.

If one grants, as I do, the central meaning and truth of the negative dialectics expressed in neo-orthodoxy, then what hope remains for any attempt—whether neo-Thomist or process—to articulate an analogical God-language? The answer to this question lies, I believe, in the unfolding of the neo-orthodox position itself. For the interesting fact is that, with the possible exception of Kierkegaard, all the major neo-orthodox theologians eventually developed analogical language for God-language without retreating from their original dialectical insights. Karl Barth's post-*Romans* turn against Kierkegaard is not, in fact, an expression of a simple fear that an existentialist philosophy will take over Christian theology. Rather, that attack is a more properly theological insistence, following upon his famous reinterpretation of Anselm, that negative dialectics alone leaves one literally no-where theologically by forcing the speaker into a mathematical point wherein Christian language for God becomes mute. As Barth works out his own "analogy of faith" language

in his *Dogmatics*, he formulates his new position consistently and
explicitly as an "analogy of faith" language for God-language with
the focal meaning of Jesus Christ.

When Paul Tillich develops his method of correlation he does not
abandon—but does transform—his earlier purely dialectical Protestant principle. For he too develops symbolic and non-symbolic (in
a word, analogical) language for God as the power of Being and Being-
Itself. That explication allows his position, in principle, to articulate
new symbolic/analogical language for God without retreating from
the insistence upon negative dialectics. When Tillich later articu-
lates the need for both Protestant principle and Catholic substance
he makes a suggestion analogous to my own: that both negative dialectics and analogy are needed for appropriate Christian God-
language.

When Rudolf Bultmann insists that theology still needs properly
analogical language to speak of God in a non-mythological manner,
even though Christian theology must eliminate mythological language in fidelity to the presence of negative dialectics in the demand of the kerygma itself, then he too recognizes the same insistence. Unlike Barth and Tillich, it is true, Bultmann never actually
developed such language as distinct from stating that it was needed.
Still, Schubert Ogden's development via Hartshorne of just such
analogical language seems, on this reading, an entirely appropriate
development of Bultmann's own position.

My own constructive suggestion for the crucial role that the neo-
orthodox theologians can play in the conversation outlined in section one can be stated in the following thesis: any Christian analogical language for God that ignores or does not incorporate the genuine anthropological and theistic insights of neo-orthodox negative
dialectics is destined for failure. More exactly stated, such non-dia-
lectical analogical language will eventually prove theologically ster-
ile by becoming, in effect, univocal or dissipating into pure equivo-
cality. The neo-Scholastic misreading of Aquinas' own dialectical
moments in his analogical language, on this reading, was not a minor misinterpretation but one fraught with fatal consequences. In a
similar manner, Charles Hartshorne's seeming lack of interest in
more than a "tragic" element in existence seems to demand the
more properly Christian theological insistence upon the presence of

more radical negative dialectical moments incorporated in both Schubert Ogden's and John Cobb's anthropological developments of Hartshorne's position.

Karl Rahner's consistent use of a dialectic of identity-in-difference in his analogical language for God assures that his reading of Aquinas, whatever its other difficulties, remains more faithful to both Aquinas and the Christian Scriptures than does the sometimes univocal, sometimes equivocal, position of his neo-Scholastic critics.

These chapters, therefore, have tried to reopen the crucial conversation about Christian theological language for God by reformulating the questions of analogy and dialectics. To recall the logic of the entire argument, the following steps are involved: the first chapter argued for the public character of theological language, including its classic systematic languages of analogy and dialectics; the second chapter outlined the character of the analogical imagination itself in order to clarify its real possibilities for discussion; the third chapter specified the major conversation partners in terms of the major similarities and differences among their finally analogical positions. If this argument is plausible, it follows that serious Christian theological speech about God will be ultimately analogical without abandoning the insights of negative dialectics. It also follows that the languages of analogy and dialectics, too long ignored of late by many Christian theologians, deserve their traditional central place in the genuinely theological discussion of God-language. For these two languages, I have come to believe, are the fully public, classic expressions of the Christian vision: a vision disclosing both the clarity and the radical mystery of our existence as grounded in and ordered to the disclosive and transformative presence of the God revealed in Christ Jesus.

CHAPTER FOUR

God and the Scientific Worldview

by John B. Cobb

Belief in God has been buffeted about in many ways in recent years. It is attacked for being meaningless, for being false, for being vapid, and for being harmful. Its defenders are in disarray. Hurrying to defend the idea from the charge of meaninglessness, we find it attacked as an error. Correcting the idea so as to show that it can be true, we are accused of trivializing it. Seeking to show that it is important, we encounter the charge that it is harmful. Clearly if what is named God is truly God, the assertion of God must be meaningful and true, and we should strive to show that God is important and good. But it is no small task to speak of God in this way.

It is easy for us who are believers to experience this buffeting and frantic defense as a gradual retreat from the great age of faith. Without doubt there are now many circles in which we find ourselves in a ghetto, either ignored or attacked, and we experience confusion and mutual criticism among ourselves. We are likely to speak of what we "still" believe, hardly expecting our children and grandchildren to hold on to these beleaguered convictions.

There is, however, another attitude that we can take. We can recognize that of all matters, thinking rightly about God is the most important. We can further note that when belief in God is general and expressions of doubt are greeted with shocked dismay and ostracism, what has been meant by "God" has not been subject to the searching scrutiny it deserves. Partly as a result, much of the worst of our heritage—as well as much of the best—has been bound up with belief in God. Therefore, we can rejoice that today the idea of God is extensively criticized on all sides. Perhaps out of the present chaos there can emerge a purer and truer understanding of God. Perhaps in this sense we can understand the manifold criticisms of theism not as obstacles or enemies, but as resources for the resolution of the problem of God.

Out of the welter of possible topics to pursue in this spirit I have chosen three: science, Buddhism, and feminism. These raise highly divergent issues for theological reflection. Science raises the question of God's relation to the world. It shows that some of our older ways of conceiving God's activity in the world do not work and that if we are to affirm God's presence in the world at all we must rethink our notions of divine agency. Buddhism raises the question of God's relation to religion. It shows that a great religious movement, a movement that produces its own saints and mystics and martyrs, is possible without belief in God. Feminism raises the question of God's relation to our images and our existence in a very intimate way. It shows that belief in God has been closely correlated with male dominance and the oppression and exploitation of women.

The challenge is now: Can we think of God in a way that is compatible with our scientific worldview without removing God's presence and efficacy from our lives and our world? Can we think of God as the one in whom we place our complete trust and yet acknowledge the truth and greatness of a Way that ignores or denies God? Can we free our thought of God from sexism without losing the profound values that have been bound up with the masculine images of God as Father and as Son?

Even if we can make progress in these directions and in others as well, we will not have proved the existence of God. Perhaps we are only adjusting ideas, not improving our thought of reality. But it is my conviction that the two are closely related. If there is a way of conceiving of God that fits with our experience of the world as that is informed by science, that illumines the encounter with other great religious traditions, and that liberates us from oppression, there will be many reasons to believe that it is true. Some of these reasons have sufficient strength to convince many people even when the objections remain unanswered. If, through this time of testing, there emerges an understanding of God that is intelligible, appropriate, relevant, and significant, and if the God who is thereby known illumines and liberates, unites and heals, reassures and challenges, the future may be a time of renewed vitality for theistic faith. These chapters will do no more than suggest a few steps in that direction.

The perspective I bring to bear on these questions is Whiteheadian. This is not for me a matter of choice. In my first year as a graduate student at the University of Chicago, my first serious exposure to modern thought, especially philosophy and psychology, shattered my previously strong conviction of the reality of God. This shattering did not take place by a frontal assault on my belief. It was more that I was drawn into a way of thinking and perceiving that was closed in on itself and that contained no place for God.

By chance, or perhaps providentially, I encountered one thinker who obviously understood modern thought far better than I and yet found it not in the least threatening to his convictions about God. His name was Charles Hartshorne, and it was clear to me that I must sit at his feet. He introduced me to a world of thought, largely Whiteheadian, that incorporated the modern vision but transcended it. In that world God gradually came alive for me again.

Now, thirty years later, I have had the chance to study more carefully the various philosophical and theological responses to the absence of God from the modern vision. I have wondered what would have become of me if at that critical time I had encountered other forms of defense of the belief in God espoused by their best proponents. And I am still not sure that any of the others would have checked my drift into atheistic modernity. At that time I could not respond to the dogmatic theology of Barth or the kerygmatic theology of Bultmann. Neither Tillich nor neo-Thomism spoke convincingly to my doubts. Boston Personalism in the form given it by E. S. Brightman challenged me, but I could not quite believe its idealism. The brilliant analyses of human nature and destiny by Reinhold Niebuhr had already moved and grasped me, but they did not deal directly with my experience of the disappearance of God. The neonaturalism that I encountered in the faculty of the Chicago Divinity School seemed to have accommodated too far to the disbelief of our age to open up for me the possibility of authentic belief. Even now, looking back, it seems that my taking the Hartshornian-

Whiteheadian direction was not the mere consequence of the chance encounter with Hartshorne. It seems more to be the one possibility of belief that was open to me in the intellectual world of the late forties.

There is a second way in which I find my Whiteheadian perspective something more than a biographical chance. The years since I was drawn into it have brought crises of faith on new grounds. Richard Rubenstein has challenged belief in a God who permitted Auschwitz and has called for return to the gods of the soil. Thomas Altizer has attacked the God of the church as repressive of human freedom and creativity and called on us, *as Christians*, to will God's death. Under the influence of dominant currents in modern philosophy many have abandoned consideration of God's reality and devoted attention to matters of language and imaging alone. The ecological crisis made us aware of how seriously our Western concentration on God has detached us from sensitive attention to our interconnectedness with all things and led us falsely to separate history from nature.

Each of these events—and the widespread cultural currents they represent and articulate—has undermined, for many, ways of conceiving of God that had survived the tension with the dominant modern worldview. It has been my experience, however, that each new challenge has made me more genuinely Whiteheadian. I have come to understand Whitehead's distaste for the image of Creator, which at first I had tried to build up, and his preference for identifying God with the tender elements that work in love. And I have come to a new appreciation of his vision of the radical interconnectedness and interdependence, even interfusion, of all things. None other, I believe, of all the ways of thinking of God propounded at the time of my own crisis of faith would have similarly flowered through the new challenges of the years ahead. I am now finding, as I wrestle with the challenges of Buddhism and feminism, that Whitehead's thought again displays heretofore untapped resources.

Let me hasten to say that I do not mean that Whitehead's doctrine of God is in itself the answer to our present and future needs. It expresses his own attention to a surprising array of the issues that have been prominent since his death. But he was not prescient or omniscient! His formulations are bound to his time and place even while, like all works of genius, they speak to other times and places as well. We need to think afresh in the light of our new experience, not to defend a doctrine formulated half a century ago. Much that I will say in these lectures cannot be found in the pages of Whitehead's writing, and if that were not true I would not be faithful to his own spirit. But in thinking afresh in new situations I find continuing and surprising help in aspects of Whitehead's vision that I had not previously noted or appreciated. Hence I find myself, inescapably, a Whiteheadian, and when I think of our common topic, "resources for the resolution of the problem of God today," I must continue to confess that for me the central resource after the Bible itself is the philosophy of Whitehead.

The remainder of this first chapter reflects my own graduate school crisis, a crisis that, I think, was typical of the experience of many Christians in the past century or more. I did not encounter arguments against belief in God. That would not have been very troublesome. Over the years I have never found arguments for or against belief in God convincing. Indeed the arguments against belief stir the debater in me, and since their weakness is easily exposed, they tend to confirm my faith. But what I did encounter was a powerful and all-encompassing way of thinking and experiencing that dominated the university in all its branches and from which God was excluded. I found this vision of reality superseding the one I had brought with me to the university. This was not a matter of choice, but a fate or destiny.

Because of the importance of this experience for me, and because I believe it is a widely shared experience, I have often reflected about it, asking what essentially made the earlier Christian vision so powerless before the modern worldview and also what is the most essential advance required beyond the modern view if theism is to be recovered on a new level. There are many answers, of course, all interrelated. For our consideration in this chapter I am choosing the theme of causality. My argument is as follows: (1) God must be the cause of something. (2) The modern view of causality excludes in principle asserting that God is the cause of anything. (3) A new view of causality opens the door to an improved understanding of how God is causally efficacious in the world.

God Must Be the Cause of Something

What God causes is subject to highly varied interpretation. Our insurance policies in their language of "acts of God" reflect a time when natural disasters were viewed as caused by God. Even today when personal disaster strikes, many people wonder why God did this to them. But there are strong theological reasons for denying this as the locus of agency of a loving God. And it accords poorly with our scientific worldview.

Others think of God as the cause of the totality of nature rather than as the particular cause of particular events. This works best when we think that nature had a beginning, and the doctrine of God as initiator of the whole show has gained some color in connection with the Big Bang theory of cosmic origins. However, God as the initiator of the Big Bang has little human meaning, and in any case it fits uncomfortably with the inevitable scientific interest in the state of nature prior to this cosmic explosion.

Accordingly, attention may be directed to humanly important features of the world as the locus of divine causality. Some have suggested that God acted to bring life into being in an inanimate world or to create human beings out of animals. But the God of the gaps recedes before scientific advance as the gaps are narrowed and the continuous character of the evolutionary development appears more and more clearly.

Finally, where the whole natural process is recognized as the sphere of science, human religious experience is sometimes identified as the place where God directly affects us. Mystical experience or faith may be singled out as phenomena that cannot be explained apart from divine causality. But, again, the advance of science can display these also as continuous with other types of phenomena in such a way that the claim that they have supernatural causes progressively decreases in plausibility.

All of these views of God's causal agency in the world are interventionist. God is seen as intervening in the nothing to initiate something and as intervening at points in the world process to effect results it would not otherwise attain. I have suggested that these views tend inevitably to retreat before the advance of science. This is not only because the gaps where God could be thought to act are becoming more narrow because of this advance, but also because the basic understanding of the world has altered. When nature was understood unhistorically as essentially changeless in its basic structure, occasional intervention to bring about new structures made some, though questionable, sense. But when nature is seen as a dynamic process, supernatural interventions are not required to account for the emergence of novel forms. Indeed the idea of an interventionist God connected with such a world makes the problem of evil insuperable. Why did God let nature spend billions of years producing what in the end requires an intervention anyway? And why did a God who acts through interventions not intervene to prevent Auschwitz?

The decline of interventionist thinking has opened the way to the development of an alternative style of theological thought. In this perspective God is a factor in all events through the spectrum of nature and history. God is sustainer, renewer, and source of directivity in the cosmic process. Life and human personhood and religious experience can be lifted up, in this perspective as well, as indicative of God's directive agency. But God's causality is seen in the whole process that produces them and follows from them rather than in individual interventions. It is God's nature to work *with* the ongoing, largely autonomous, process continuously rather than at occasional discreet moments. Hence we are led to attend to our present and ordinary experiences rather than to focus on a few "mighty works."

This mode of conceiving of God is not vulnerable to scientific advance in the way that interventionist modes of thinking are. Nevertheless, it too faces acute problems. Often God's efficacy is indicated so vaguely that God cannot be distinguished from the natural process as a whole and appears simply to be brought in for rhetorical purposes. If, on the other hand, God's causal agency in the process is seriously affirmed, we confront the fact that modern reflection on causality rules out this possibility in advance.

The Modern Understanding of Causality Excludes God's Causality in Principle

This was certainly not true for Isaac Newton. In his thought entities acted upon other entities according to imposed laws. God was the author of these laws and the agency of their imposition. God was, thus, not one cause among others, but the cause of the laws that regulate all other causal relations. It is the erosion of the Newtonian vision that has made talk of God problematic in the modern scientific worldview.

Hume is the key figure in this erosion. He called attention to the fact that we never observe causal connections except as regularity of contiguous succession between phenomena. A law is a generalization of such regularities. Hume denied that a law is imposed, and, hence, saw no need of a divine law-giver.

In this perception, a cause is an antecedent member in an observed regular succession. In principle, therefore, the cause must be observable. Also it must be a phenomenon that sometimes occurs and sometimes does not. God clearly cannot be a cause in this sense. God is not sensuously observable, and God is not an occasional phenomenon.

Hume's view has been widely contested but, in modified versions, it has become the orthodoxy against which critics must contend. This remains true even when the shift of focus from metaphysics to logic leads to a shift from consideration of cause to consideration of explanation. An occurrence is explained when its relation to antecedent states of affairs is subsumed under a law that is a generalization of such observed relations. With this doctrine of explanation it is impossible to explain any feature of the observable world by reference to something in principle unobservable, for example, God.

The difficulty created for theism by this modern understanding of causality and explanation can hardly be exaggerated. Both theoretically and practically the reasons for affirming God have always been the judgment of the need to affirm a cause. This has been articulated as the principle of sufficient reason, that is, there must be a sufficient reason for the occurrence of whatever occurs. There are many features of the world for which antecedent circumstances, however regular, do not appear to be sufficient reasons. This leads to explaining them as God-given. In this way we were encouraged to reason from effect to cause. But the more deeply we are drawn into the dominant modern vision, the less free we find ourselves to think in such terms. For this modern vision, we can reason only from cause to effect; we cannot reason from effect to cause. The logical form of explanation is identical with the logical form of prediction.

One may argue that the replacement of the principle of sufficient reason with the covering law model of explanation is simply arbitrary and can therefore be rejected by theists. In a sense this is true. No one has ever refuted the principle of sufficient reason or proved the exclusive correctness of covering law explanation. But such a response is completely inadequate, for to appeal to God as the cause or explanation of some aspect of the world is unconvincing unless what is meant by cause and explanation is itself explained. If the Humean model of causality is rejected, with what can it be replaced?

A New View of Causality Opens the Door to an Improved Understanding of How God Is Causally Efficacious in the World

What Hume missed in the causal relations he observed was any inherent necessity or, we might say in a commonsense way, any causality. He could observe successive events, and he believed that once the former occurred the latter would follow, but he could not observe any production by the first of the second. The relation of the two events appeared to be external to both of them.

Now if for all other purposes the view of cause as regular succession proved satisfying, it would be a fruitless move to propose a different mode of causality for the sake of theism. But this is far from the case. There is a large literature, for example, arguing that the explanations of events sought by historians are quite different from Humean explanations, and even in the hard sciences covering law theory has acute difficulties with, for example, statistical laws. Indeed, it seems that the only reason for clinging to the Humean view is that in the realm of public events experienced through the senses there is no other way to go. Sensa are of necessity susceptible only to external relations.

The original home of causal thinking was quite elsewhere. In the Greek law courts one sought to determine the cause of a crime, that on which it was to be blamed, as a precondition of appropriate punishment. Today it is necessary to return to the human sphere for a new model of causality.

In personal, subjective experience we are all aware of causes as something more than regular succession. If someone grabs my arm and forces me to move it against my will, I am aware of being compelled to move my arm. If I decide to write a word and then write it, I experience myself writing because of the decision, not merely following it. If my tooth aches, I feel the throbbing in the tooth as the cause of my experience of pain. In all these cases the relation of the two events is not merely external. It is internal to the later event, which occurs not only after the other event but because of it. The cause is internal to or contained in the effect.

Let me offer one more example. I would not be writing this if I did not hope to influence the readers in some measure. To influence is to flow into. My hope is that some of the ideas I am expressing and perhaps even some of my verbal formulations will flow into the readers, that is, become part of them. That would not necessarily mean that they accepted all my ideas, but it would mean the ideas entered the readers' experience for reflective consideration and judgment. The relation of my ideas to a reader's experience would not be a matter of regular temporal succession. It would be a matter of participation in the constitution of the reader's experience.

Internal relations are involved in all genuinely causal relations. If the reader's experience is affected by the writer's ideas, this is because these ideas in some measure become a constitutive part of the reader's experience. It is true that a third party cannot observe this internalization and insofar as the third party position is the basis for science, this internal relation lies outside the scientific vision. The scientific observer would be limited to observing the reader's behavior and seeking correlations between it and the written words. But this would not be the primary causal relationship, which is immediately available only to the attentive reader.

When causality is understood as regular succession, one cannot reason from the effect to the cause since the cause is external to the effect; that is, the effect bears no witness to the cause. The same effect could have arisen from another cause. But when causality is understood as the internalization of the antecedent event by a consequent one, as in the case of one person grasping the meaning of

another, the situation is quite different. Here we cannot predict the
effect from the cause, for there is no necessity that readers attend
to ideas even if they read a book. But if the effect occurs—if ideas
are assimilated—the cause can be inferred. Of course, there can be
mistakes in such inference, but without risking such reasoning, and
apart from its general reliability, life could not go on. We experience our pain as arising from events in the body and we adjust ourselves accordingly. We could not survive if we simply experienced
the pain or the words and required knowledge of Humean laws to
identify their causes. There are times when knowledge of Humean
laws is helpful, but people remove their hands from hot stoves *before* they learn generalizations about heat causing pain.

Now I am claiming that this kind of causality we all know so well
provides a much better way of conceiving of God's causality in the
world than do either Newtonian or Humean notions. It implies that
God is efficacious in the world to the extent that worldly events
include God within them. This inclusion does not determine just
how they will constitute themselves any more than a reader's inclusion of a writer's suggestions determines how the reader will respond. But the inclusion makes a difference, and a very important
difference.

Thus far I have argued for three points. First, to talk about God
is to talk of God as the cause of something, and it is far better to
think of this something as an aspect of all events rather than to think
of God's causal efficacy in terms of intervention in an otherwise autonomous course of events. Second, the modern, dominantly Humean, understanding of causality excludes any notion of God's causal
efficacy in the world. Third, through the analysis of the root experiences of causality we can arrive at an understanding of the cause
as participating in the constitution of the effect, and this understanding leaves open the possibility that God, too, participates in
the constitution of events in the world.

If it makes sense to think of God as causally effective in the world,
the remaining question is whether there is evidence in the world of
such effectiveness. Are there human experiences of God's grace,
power, or efficacy? Or, more generally, are there aspects of experience that are best explained through affirming the effective presence of God as their cause?

That many people believe that they have had experiences of God
goes without question. That the unobservability of God as cause
does not in itself render such beliefs fallacious is now also clear. That
the causal relation of God to the world stands outside of the work of
science need not disturb us. Still there are reasons for serious doubt.

We know that there are errors in identifying the cause even in
the clearest and most vivid experiences. For most of us most of the
time the experience of God's grace and agency in our lives is not
clear and vivid. There has been much error in adjudging various
aspects of experience as God's grace, and we worry that we too may
be in error. Where there is so little clarity, we suspect that the
whole tendency to interpret experience in terms of God's agency
may be derived from cultural convention and wishful thinking. There
are, on the other hand, experiences felt so powerfully as experiences of God that the subjects know them to be such, and the understanding of causality I have proposed can sometimes justify them
in their conviction. But even their assurance requires some notion
of God and God's agency that does not transform these experiences
into eccentricities but sees them as the heightening and enlivening
of God's presence everywhere. Hence we need to consider philo-
sophically what role God may be thought to play in the total process
to provide a context for the appreciation of those most vivid experiences. Where there is no vivid consciousness of God's presence as
such, what features of the world may we most reasonably suppose
are the result of his presence?

I propose that we consider freedom to be such a feature. We can
approach this through a brief examination of the recent philosophical discussions of freedom. These arise generally from the fact that
philosophers know that we do attribute responsibility to people for
at least some of their actions. The question is whether this is justi-
fied and, if so, why.

One position is that the view that people are responsible for their
actions is false. The more we understand actions psychologically and
sociologically and even physically and chemically the more we realize that there are reasons for just those actions. Given the conditions, the total situation, only that action could occur. There may be
reasons for punishing some actions as a means of introducing new
causal factors into the future situation, but there is no sense in

speaking of justice, as if a murderer "deserved" punishment. That appeals only to primitive instincts of revenge. The act of murdering followed necessarily from the situation just as an act of kindness might follow necessarily from a slightly different situation. This position is called hard determinism.

The difficulty with hard determinism is that it is inconsistent with so much of our ordinary language and common sense. We hold people responsible for what they do in our law courts and in ordinary life in ways that conflict with the implications of hard determinism. Of course, that does not refute hard determinism as a metaphysical position, but it does show why philosophers who orient themselves to ordinary language, as so many have done in recent years, find it an uncomfortable doctrine. They have devised an alternative position known as soft determinism.

The soft determinists stress that we can and do make distinctions between what we are compelled to do and what we do freely. What we do freely is what we do because of our own intentions and desires. They think it is possible to explain why we intend or desire what we do. Hence a free action can be explained just as well as one that is forced upon us. This explanation will show that it too is determined. But when the act is determined by our own purposes, we are responsible. When the act is forced upon us, we are not.

Soft determinism certainly comes closer to describing the way we do think about responsibility than does hard determinism. However, the hard determinists rightly point out that on the basic questions there is no difference. If I act from my purpose, but my purpose, directly or indirectly, is a function of physical and chemical or sociological or historical conditions, then I am still not responsible in any serious sense. If the courts choose to use this distinction as a basis for determining my legal guilt, there is nothing to prevent them. But responsibility of this sort cannot justify moral judgments.

There are other philosophers who reject determinism altogether. They point out that from a Humean point of view determinism is no more than a faith that every aspect of every event can ultimately be brought under general laws. Many recommend this as a good attitude to adopt so that we will not stop the search for such general laws at any point. But since laws relate only to types of events or aspects of events, not to events in their totality, it is hard to see how any event in its concrete determinateness could ever be brought exhaustively under covering laws. Hence there is no logical basis for excluding a measure of indeterminateness.

Indeterminacy, however, does not imply responsibility. As the Stoics recognized long ago, the fact that some of our actions are not determined would mean that we do not determine them. For an action that I do not determine, I cannot be held accountable.

Does this mean that in fact our basic notions of freedom and responsibility are illusory? This is the general impression one receives from reading recent philosophic discussions. Either an action is determined or it is not determined, and in neither case can we intelligibly attribute to it the sort of responsibility we associate with freedom.

The only alternative seems to be to introduce an additional category: self-determination. Now self-determination can be understood as nothing more than what the soft determinist asserts, that is, that among the immediately precipitating factors behind an act a key one was the person's own intention. But self-determination must mean more than that if it is to help us out of our quandary. It must mean that the intention was not in its turn a product of antecedent factors alone. Instead the intention must have been in part self-determined in the moment in which it precipitated the action.

To think clearly about what is asserted here, we should consider the moment of human experience in which the intention is formed. What must be asserted is that although this moment of experience arose out of a complex past that deeply affected it, it had some autonomy in its constitution of itself. That is, this momentary experience must not be simply an outgrowth of its past, and features in it that are not determined by the past must not be simply a matter of chance. The act of experience must in some measure determine itself. Only thus can it be responsible in an ethically intelligible way for itself or for the overt actions to which it leads.

This is a difficult idea for most philosophers. Part of the difficulty stems from the fact that such self-determination presupposes multiple possibilities. Also these possibilities must include possibilities not realized in the effective antecedent world. But for the dominant modern vision the antecedent world at any point exhausts reality. Nothing can enter a moment of experience from anywhere else since there is nowhere else. Hence multiple possibilities cannot really present themselves, and self-determination in this radical sense is impossible.

The alternative is to argue that since self-determination is real, the antecedent world does not exhaust reality. There is also the sphere of possibility which presents itself as effectively relevant for decision in each moment. The moment of experience constitutes itself out of its antecedent world, but how it responds to that world— what, in its self-constitution, it does with that world—is affected by the new possibilities among which it chooses.

The question remains: how can possibilities unrealized in the antecedent world attain effective relevance for the new moment of experience? This is a complicated way of asking our basic question: how can there be real freedom? And the answer is that in addition to the antecedent world there is also another reality that enters into each moment opening up a space of self-determination. The other reality is God.

Let me summarize the argument. We experience ourselves as free. If we are truly free, that means that the way we constitute ourselves transcends the sheer outworking of the past. This means that there are possibilities genuinely available for realization that are not contributed by the past world. These possibilities must be felt as such in the process of self-constitution. Since nothing in the past world can be the cause of the effectiveness of these possibilities, that cause transcends the world. It is appropriate to call it God. To think of God as the cause of the effectiveness of these possibilities is to think of God as a factor in the self-constitution of each experience, for this is what it means to be a cause. According to our earlier consideration of causality, to think of God as the cause of the effectiveness of new possibilities—and thus the cause of freedom— is to think of God as participating in the constitution of experience. Or to put it more personally, it is by virtue of the presence of God that I experience a call to be more than I have been and more than my circumstances necessitate that I be. It is that call to transcendence that frees me from simply acting by habit and reacting to the forces of the world. In short, it is by God's grace that I am free.

I have not, of course, proved the existence of God. I cannot even prove that freedom is real. Determinists see the same world and are convinced that everything is as it must be because its past is what it is. Whatever phenomenon I may point to as indicating that the present transcends the past, determinists will claim that in time an explanation can be given that shows that there has been no such transcendence. Against that claim there can be no proof, only the witness of our ordinary language and the deep-seated conviction that something more occurs than the unrolling of what is preestablished and predetermined. What I have tried to show is that belief in freedom and belief in God belong together, and that—once we are free to think in terms of non-Humean causality and explanation—it makes sense to refer to God as the explanation of our freedom.

Furthermore, the association of freedom with God is not a convenient ad hoc solution to our current difficulties with theism. It is an ancient connection. As a sweeping generalization over the history of religions and associated philosophies, I think it can be safely said that creative freedom and personal responsibility have been accented where belief in the biblical God has been alive. Human freedom has not been a topic of reflection in Oriental philosophy and religion, and although its roots can be found in Greek thought, the theme was not fully articulated or clarified. Discussion of human freedom has withered in the philosophy that most fully reflects the dominant modern worldview. But where the biblical God was understood to hold before human beings new possibilities for their lives—indeed a new historical order, and finally a new world—there human beings have experienced themselves as free to transcend the bounds of the past and to live from the not yet realized possibilities.

This historical connection of freedom and God has been appreciated even by some atheists, such as Ernst Bloch. But it must be admitted that there are those who affirm freedom in our world without seeing any need to speak of God. This has been possible chiefly because, alongside the kind of philosophy I have been describing, dominant in the Anglo-American world, there has been an idealist way of thinking that long ago responded to the challenge of science in quite a different manner. The idealists rightly saw that science omitted from its consideration the scientist and indeed all human knowing. Since science is a production of human beings, they insisted that the primary reality is the human one. The characteristics of the human mind that make knowledge possible are logically and metaphysically prior to the information that science contributes. Hence what is to be said of human beings, such as whether or not they are free, is in no way restricted by the scientific attitude or findings. Phenomenology and existentialism represent the last great expressions of this idealist spirit. Where that prevails human freedom can be taken as a starting point requiring no defense and no explanation. Indeed any explanation appears as a concession to an inappropriate demand and even as an infringement upon the freedom itself.

I rejoice in this bold affirmation of freedom as we find it, for example, in Jean-Paul Sartre. It witnesses to the strength of the inner certainty of freedom where this is not eroded by restrictive ideas of what is possible. But I also believe that the radical dualism of the human consciousness and the physical world that freed Sartre from all need of explanation is itself eroding. It becomes increasingly difficult to suppose that consciousness is in no way to be explained by physiology, that consciousness and the body belong to different spheres such that each is to be understood without regard for the other. Merleau-Ponty, from the phenomenological side, began the process of correlating consciousness with the lived body, that is, the body as inwardly experienced. Now, in the structuralism that has risen to prominence in France—partly displacing phenomenology and extentialism—the deterministic perspective encouraged by science intrudes sharply into the explanation of human experience. This course of thought suggests that the sheer affirmation of radical freedom—based on immediate experience but cut off from belief in God—will some day appear as a residue of an earlier faith, unable to sustain itself for long.

There is a final point to be made about freedom, and it is a point that atheistic affirmers of freedom have found most difficult. Significant freedom requires that in the process of self-determination the distinction of better and worse be experienced as a real and relevant factor. This should not be thought of in the first instance as an ethical question. Moral distinctions may or may not play a role. But in a significant act of self-determination, of deciding among possibilities, there must be some felt ranking of these possibilities. It must be better to realize some rather than others, otherwise the choice is arbitrary and freedom cannot be felt as significant.

Sartre struggled against this conclusion. He even argued that for freedom to be truly free we must decide what is better and worse with no antecedent standards by which to decide. He was opposing chiefly, of course, the idea of moral rules of conduct imposed upon us by society or God, which we heteronomously obey or disobey. And of course he is right that any significant freedom must be freedom to decide whether such rules are themselves good or evil. But his formulations were far more extreme than that, for his philosophy allowed him no norm in relation to freedom that was not freely, and hence arbitrarily, chosen. Actually he qualified this extreme claim in various ways, whether legitimately or not, for he strongly believed that we should exercise freedom so as to maximize the freedom of others rather than to enslave them, and he did not really believe that to act by that principle was arbitrary.

In the moment of decision the decision loses significance if it is not immediately felt that some modes of self-constitution are truly, in themselves, better than others; for example (as with Sartre) those that enhance freedom rather than reduce it. But that means that in the giving of freedom God gives also the call to its fullest exercise. God does not simply open up a space for our self-determination. God also urges or lures us to use that freedom to the fullest—to eschew, for example, those easy decisions to neglect our new possibilities for the sake of safer reiteration of past habits. God is thus not only the giver of freedom, but also the call to be more free. And finally the ethical element does enter. For God's call is not only that we so determine ourselves as to be more free, but also that we constitute ourselves so as to contribute to the freedom of others. Our experience of God is an experience of an ideal, not a fixed ideal, but a new one moment by moment—an ideal possibility for realization in that situation pulling us away from the easy out, the slothful capitulation to inertia. We are aware, at the deepest level of our being, that there are possibilities of good that we partly realize and partly miss, and in that awareness we experience the immanence of God in our lives.

CHAPTER FIVE

God and Buddhism

by John B. Cobb

In the preceding chapter I argued that to believe ourselves free and to experience that freedom as a gift of God conflicts in no way with the fullest development of science, although it does conflict with a worldview that tries to extrapolate directly from modern scientific methods and habits of mind. This approach, I suggest, is not a trick to escape into an area where science cannot follow, but a contemporary reaffirmation of the early Christian vision that intimately associated belief in God and the experience and affirmation of human freedom. Modern determinism is analogous to the classical fatalism from which the Christian affirmation of God liberated the Mediterranean world.

Neither the reality of freedom nor the reality of God is proved by this connection, but we who experience both are free to clarify our faith through the encounter with modern science and its associated worldview. In doing so we see how often our tradition has demeaned God by speaking of God as one cause alongside others in the world, or else as the exclusive cause of rare events. We can be grateful to science, for the clarification of God as the giver of freedom is not a restriction to a narrow realm but an opportunity to understand that realm as the all-important one, the true locus of all human creativity. We can now see that the desire to attribute ordinary efficient causality to God was an expression of a lack of faith. It is the insistence that Elijah should have seen God in the fire and whirlwind and that Jesus should have yielded to Satan's temptations in the wilderness. It may well be the reason that the church has too often yielded to analogous temptations. It is through the gift of freedom that God has brought into the world life, consciousness, the passion for truth, free associations of peoples, and communities of love.

In this chapter I want to confront this response to the scientific challenge with the challenge that arises in the study of the history of religions. Westerners have often supposed that we know what religion in general is all about through our own experience of religion. We think we can distinguish the particular features of our religion from what is common to all. In the light of this comparison, some Westerners have preferred to strip our Western traditions of their special or "positive" features, which they suppose are all that distinguish them from "pure" religion. Others have felt that these positive features make our Western religions superior to all others.

Belief in God has often been viewed as one of the features common to all religions. Indeed, the supposed universality of the hunger for God has been a factor strengthening the conviction that God is not a cultural projection but a reality that impinges on all human life. Of course it is recognized that God is known under many names, and that the unity of God is often not recognized. But it is assumed, nonetheless, that God may be found within the belief structure of all peoples.

To a point this expectation has been vindicated in the study of the world's religious traditions. Divine or sacred beings play a role in primitive religions everywhere, and as these are transformed into the great traditional Ways of humankind, this early stage leaves its mark on popular piety. Nevertheless, outside of the Western religions nurtured in Judaism, it is hard to find the Christian God under other names. It is equally hard to find analogous attention to what the Christian knows as freedom.

If we look at others of the great Ways for support of our belief in God, the situation is disturbing. It is true that all religions witness to some sense of the sacred. But it is not true that in their dominant theoretical expressions they all witness to a sacred reality significantly analogous to the Western God. It seems that belief in God, as we understand that in the West, has arisen chiefly from the Jewish and Western experience, not from a universally human one.

That judgment seems to confirm another widespread view of Eastern religions as "heathen." If their practitioners do not even know God, how important it is that we teach them and bring them to faith! But it is now too late in our history to judge Asian Ways inferior simply because they are profoundly different. They have probed the human depths with remarkable penetration and seen much that we in the West have neglected. Yet they have not found God.

I have stated this conclusion strongly. It is, in relation to the Eastern Ways, a matter of dispute. For example, some scholars believe that what Confucianists call Heaven expresses their experience of the reality Westerners call God. Some scholars translate the Hindu Brahman as God or identify God with Isvara. Alternatively, one may suppose that the distinction of Brahman and Isvara reflects the incompleteness of Indian thought compared with the unity of their characteristics in the Christian God.

The pursuit of this kind of question is itself fruitful for Western reflection about the meaning of the word God. That one person may identify Brahman as God and another, Isvara, and that one may see the Confucian Heaven as God, while another disagrees, can be taken at first as a debate about how Brahman, Isvara, and Heaven are to be rightly understood. But on fuller analysis, it turns out instead to be a debate about the essential characteristics of God. Is God fundamentally the ultimate sacred reality underlying and manifesting itself in all things? Or is God the personal object of trust and loving devotion? Or, again, is God the source of natural and social order? Until recently our Western habit has been to attribute all this and more to God with little discrimination. In the context of the history of religion, this will no longer do, and we see that in our own traditions God has named diverse aspects of reality. It is no longer clear that the God of Thomistic metaphysics and the Father of Jesus Christ are the same reality.

As a result we are no longer sure what is at stake in debates about the existence of God. Does the denial of God at one blow deny the Hindu Brahman, the Confucian Heaven, the Thomistic Being, and the Father of Jesus Christ? That would be, indeed, a sweeping denial. Or does it deny only a supernatural, anthropomorphic, Newtonian, interventionist deity? That would be much simpler, and many believers in the Hindu Brahman, the Confucian Heaven, the Thomistic Being, and the Father of Jesus Christ will share that denial.

So the question of God is wide open today as it has never been before. Perhaps our question today is not whether or not we believe in God but how we understand inclusive reality and whether within that understanding we find it appropriate to designate the whole or some element as God. Because of our uncertainty as to the essential meaning of the word, two persons viewing reality alike might reach opposite decisions as to whether to affirm God. We need to work toward some criteria of continuity with past usage by which to guide this decision, if the chaos is not to destroy the remnant of communication still aided by talk of God. This clarification must today take place in the context of the history of religions.

I have omitted Buddhism from the above considerations. Especially in the form of Zen, Buddhism constitutes a challenge to Western theism.

Even in the study of Zen, both Western and Buddhist scholars have at times found it useful to translate certain Buddhist notions as God. But here, more clearly than in any other tradition, Westerners find themselves confronted with a drive beyond anything that could for them represent God. Buddhists like to see in Meister Eckhart a Western mystic who shared in part their experience. However, it is not Eckhart's God, but his Godhead, that appeals to them, and even this seems to be dissolved in the ultimate reaches of Buddhist experience. Even by the broadest stretching of our notion of God, it is hardly possible to identify Nirvana, the goal of Buddhist striving, with God.

Just as many Christians want to see in all religions a quest for God, so many Buddhists want to see in all religions, at their purest, the movement toward that Nothingness or Emptiness that is completed and perfected in their own experience. They prefer to see in the Western thought of God an incompletely demythologized and desubstantialized notion through which, nonetheless, sensitive persons have moved on through negation to Nirvana. If, as I believe, study of the history of religions shows that what the West means by God is no more a halfway house to Nirvana than what the Buddhist means by Nirvana is a distortion of what the West means by God, then there will be disappointed Buddhists just as there will be disappointed Christians.

If the hands of Christians and Buddhists extended from each side

out of a sense of common purpose must fall back to their sides un-
grasped, there seems to be a reason for sadness. But perhaps the
gift that each can give the other is more precious even than compan-
ionship on a common path. Perhaps each can learn from the other
something that it has not yet learned from its own history but to
which it may now be open.

This mutual instruction is possible, of course, only if the deep
differences between Christian and Buddhist thought do not amount
to contradictions. If Buddhists necessarily deny the reality of the
God in which Christians necessarily believe, then there can only be
competition and conflict between them, and there is much evidence
in favor of this view. Nevertheless, both Buddhism and Christianity
are and express modes of experience, and modes of experience in
themselves cannot contradict each other. They may, of course, be
very divergent and may give rise to mutually contradictory beliefs.
But the most accurate interpretation of such divergent experiences
should be free of contradiction. Hence, however different, it should
be possible to formulate Buddhist and Christian beliefs in noncon-
tradictory ways.

The technical possibility of noncontradiction between Christian
and Buddhist teaching would not do away with conflict. It may be
that attention to the Christian God prevents the realization of Nothingness, and that the realization of Nothingness makes trust in God
impossible. But if this mutual incompatibility is not grounded in
contradiction, then the question of whether it, too, might be transcended is still open. The self-development required to be a cham-
pion weight lifter and that required to be a professional pianist are
profoundly different. The two may be forever imcompatible, but
that remains an empirical question.

It is my Christian hope that it may be possible for Christians to
realize Nothingness without ceasing to trust in God. I am told by
some Buddhists that this is impossible, that trusting in God is a
clinging that must be let go. My first goal is to show that this is an
empirical question. If so, then those who without ceasing to be
Christian are seeking to become Buddhists too may show the way
forward in practice as I try to do in theory.

To appraise the challenge of Buddhism to our belief in God, we
will first need to look more closely at Buddhism and at its central

tenet, Nirvana. This doctrine has fascinated and appalled Western students of Buddhism. Nirvana means extinction, as in the blowing out of a candle, and this notion is applied to the human self as its highest good. Most Western scholars in the past were convinced that Nirvana could not mean simply extinction of self. For them, the extinction of self could only mean death, and specifically death that led to nothing more. They could not believe that hundreds of millions of people have devoted themselves to that goal. Hence they insisted that although some philosophic systematizations of Buddhism did indeed teach extinction, original and popular Buddhism offered a way of achieving a tranquil and serene happiness undisturbed by anxiety and guilt. At death the one who had achieved enlightenment would enter into a blessed immortality. With this understanding Buddhism could have great attraction to the West as it sought a positive religious faith free from the supernaturalism and legalism that were associated with the Christian God.

Other scholars recognized that this interpretation was a projection of Western ideals upon the texts. The texts spoke of annihilation rather than immortality. Still this annihilation was not simply identical with death as total extinction. It was rather the dissolution of the personal ego. But it remained perplexing to Westerners in general how this could be the goal sought so diligently by so many people.

Today we speak readily of altered states of consciousness. This provides us with much better access to the understanding of Buddhism. Although in the nineteenth century such talk was rare and difficult for Westerners to understand, the German philosopher Arthur Schopenhauer did grasp Buddhism in this way. Schopenhauer's own sense of reality had affinities with Buddhism that were nourished by his reading of Buddhist texts. He believed that the phenomenal world is a product of the human will, that this world is fundamentally characterized by suffering, and that salvation can only consist in the extinction of the will. This extinction is so basic a change that we can form no notion of what life is like when it has occurred, but we can glimpse the positive character of the results in the lives of mystics. Buddhism, Schopenhauer believed, was a system designed to produce this radical alteration of human reality.

Unfortunately, Schopenhauer's interpretation had little influence. Although the analogy with Western mysticism was considered by others, it meant for them nothing other than union with God. Hence, insofar as Buddhist Nirvana was interpreted as mystical experience, it could be seen as the Buddhist name for deity, or as the way of describing union with God.

Western mysticism has continued to be the best bridge to the understanding of Buddhism in the twentieth century. D. T. Suzuki, the leading Buddhist interpreter of Buddhism to the English-speaking world, spoke unabashedly of Buddhism as Eastern mysticism and even spoke of Nirvana as God. He could point to a long tradition in the West of the *via negativa*, that is, the path to God through negation of everything we can know and think. This is associated with negative language about God as Nothing, and of crucifying and emptying ourselves so that we may be united with this Nothing. He insisted that even in its most extreme forms Western mysticism did not go far enough, but he saw that it moved toward Nirvana.

At this point the Westerner who admires Buddhism is forced to note a critical problem. The features of Western mysticism which move furthest in the direction Buddhists advocate are just those that have been viewed with greatest discomfort by the vast majority of the Christian community. These features seem to arise historically more from the influence of Neoplatonism than from the Bible. They subordinate or annihilate the personal God and transcend the distinctions of right and wrong, better or worse. Thus, in finding a bridge of understanding between East and West, it is to the heresies of Christianity that the Buddhist turns rather than to its mainstream of faith in God.

If we should agree that Nirvana is the Buddhist name for the reality we have called God, the results would be disconcerting. There is little doubt that Buddhist accounts of Nirvana arise from deep, existential experience. They cannot be dismissed as speculations. Their account reflects with greater consistency the indications arising from some of the greater mystics of the West. But in the perspective of this experience all that the Bible speaks of as God disappears. The conclusion seems to be that the Bible is a primitive book based on superficial experience, that we should turn from the God of the Bible to the true God who is better named Nirvana.

This conclusion is not acceptable to Christians so long as they remain Christians. Thomas Merton, one of the great Catholic mystics of this century, felt the powerful attraction of Buddhism and set out to incorporate Buddhist spirituality into his own life. His conclusion was that Buddhism is a superb means of leading us into purity of heart which is the first stage of the mystical experience, but that we must turn to Christian resources to proceed to its highest development. In his own words: "Purity of heart establishes man in a state of unity and emptiness in which he is one with God. But this is the necessary preparation . . . for the real work of God which is revealed in the Bible, the work of the *new creation,* the resurrection from the dead, the restoration of all things in Christ." *(Zen and the Birds of Appetite,* New York: New Directions, 1948, p. 132.) Needless to say, Buddhists reject this, convinced that one who could think of going beyond Nirvana to something else has simply not understood Nirvana. Are we reduced here to an argument between two types of mysticism, each holding that the other has failed to penetrate the One Reality with sufficient depth?

There is another and more fruitful possibility that requires profound rethinking of the Christian God. God has been conceived in the West as the One Ultimate Reality, the Absolute. It is obvious that this is not biblical language, but it has been characteristic of Christians that as they encountered new language that seemed to exalt God they have readily appropriated it. In the process some distinctive features of the biblical witness to God have been blurred.

For example, the Bible always distinguishes God and the world. In Genesis God's creation is depicted as the ordering of a primal chaos that is distinct from God. God is depicted as having power over the chaos, that is, power to order it purposefully, but the creatures who express the divine purposes remain other than God. They have their own being as forms of order constituted out of the chaos. They can obey or disobey God.

In its doctrine of creation out of nothing, the church remained faithful to most of this picture. It retained the idea that the substance or matter of the creatures was radically distinct from God. But in relation to the Genesis account it exaggerated the unilateral power of God. Instead of picturing God as ordering chaotic matter, it pictures God as transforming nothing into that matter in the act of giving it form. Since the very matter of the creature exists only at the divine pleasure, the autonomy of the creature is undercut. The Genesis account pictures God as vastly powerful over the creatures, able to expel them from paradise and order their new lives. The church's account makes this power absolute.

As a result of this absolutization of God's power beyond anything stated in the Bible, the reality of evil in the world has become a mystery and the justification of God's ways has become impossible. In the Genesis account Adam and Eve were agents who could obey God or yield to temptation. There is no suggestion that their disobedience was itself a direct expression of God's power. From this perspective it is possible to think of God's creative work as very good while recognizing how profoundly it has been corrupted by human disobedience. The creation would not be good if the creatures had no autonomous being and power. With this creative power the creatures are able to be destructive of much that is good and to deny themselves the happiness that would accompany obedience. But when God's power is considered absolute—when, that is, there can be no autonomy over against God—then human sin as well as all other evil must be viewed as embodying the will and purpose of God. If, in spite of this, God is believed to be good, then the world with all its horrors must be, in Leibniz' famous phrase, "the best of all possible worlds."

The movement of absolutizing God at the expense of the world did not stop there. The church thought that if God is Ultimate Reality, then God must be the ultimate reality of all things. That is, in fact, consistent with the view that God is the sole power, for as Plato saw long ago, to be real is to exercise some power. If the world exercises no power in relation to God than it has no reality distinct from God. This means that such reality as the world has is God's reality, and this can be expressed by asserting that all being derives from God and is finally identical with God. In sum, God is Being or Being Itself. This is clearly a profoundly different view of God from that offered in Genesis or, for that matter, anywhere in the Bible. Its implications were worked out with some consistency by Spinoza. Within the mainstream of Christianity, thinkers resisted these pantheistic tendencies in loyalty to Scripture. They have dealt with the resulting tension subtly and often brilliantly, but we may speculate that one reason leadership in original thought about God and the world passed out of the hands of theologians in modern times is that they committed themselves to holding together two sets of ideas whose true synthesis could not be realized. To this day most philosophical critiques of Christianity play upon the incapacity of theologians to reconcile the irreconcilable elements in the tradition.

Our concern here is with mystical experience. In Meister Eckhart we have a clear case of the realization of the implications of the duality in Christian theology. On the one hand, deity was the personal God of the Old Testament and the Father of Jesus Christ. On the other hand, deity was identified as the ultimate reality of all things, that is, as Being itself. Officially, they were one and the same God. But Eckhart in his mystical experience knew that they were not. Being, as such, Eckhart called the Godhead. To realize this deity Eckhart could plunge deep into his own being. For such a movement Eckhart did not need the personal God whose reality he also knew and revered. Godhead as Being is found equally in all that is, in the human person as well as in the personal God. God and humans are alike embodiments of this one deity.

These conclusions violate the deepest intentions of the Genesis account and even of the church's first exaggeration of the power of God. Theologians had attributed sole power to the biblical personal God in order to exalt. But a personal God must be a relational God and the power of a personal God must be power to act in relation to others who have some autonomy. Power over what is wholly powerless is not power at all. By attempting to exalt God's power into omnipotence, that is, *all* power, they denied that God's power could be exercised on anything other than God's own power; in this way they emptied the notion of power of all meaning. Omnipotence in this sense can be attributed only to the whole or to the being of the whole. Omnipotence leads logically either to pantheism or to the identification of God with what Eckhart knew as Godhead. When that move has been made the personal God to whom omnipotence was first attributed becomes only a powerless expression of the One Ultimate Reality, Being Itself, or, in profounder apprehension, Nothingness. Finally, the notion of power itself disappears.

Instead of seeking in Buddhism of the Zen variety an equivalent of the Christian God, we do better to use the encounter with Buddhism as an occasion for recovering the biblical God from the distortions that have resulted from heaping supposed metaphysical compliments upon God. Of course, that cannot mean that we simply deny that God is in some way ultimate. The biblical God is ultimate. And for me it does not mean that we should avoid philosophy or even metaphysics. What the encounter with Buddhism encourages us to do is to reopen the question of what it means to be ultimate. It may be that the biblical God is ultimate in some respects and not in others, and that the effort to treat God as ultimate in all respects destroyed the fundamental biblical vision.

In the first chapter I pointed out that God's reality must be the reason or explanation of some feature of our world. Otherwise there is no point in talking about God. Such explanation need not be in terms of efficient causation. It can also be in terms of material, formal, and final causation. For Aristotle there is no ultimate in the chain of efficient causation, and God is the ultimate in the line of formal and final causes. Aristotle was least interested in pursuing the question of material causes, and it was left to later Aristotelians to name the ultimate material cause "prime matter." Certainly Aristotle would not have thought it appropriate to view God as the ultimate material cause!

It is equally clear that the Bible does not view God as the material cause of the world. God is not the answer to the question *what* the world is but rather to the questions why the world is, how it came into being, and continues in being, and to what end it is directed. To these questions God is the ultimate answer, and this answer is confused and finally destroyed when, in the attempt to honor God, God is identified with Being as such, the ultimate Western answer to the question *what* the world is.

When we turn to Buddhism we find explicit and insistent rejection of the questions to which the God of the Bible is the answer. According to Buddhists we must cease to reflect on why the world is, how it came into being, what sustains it in being, and to what end it is directed. We must concentrate all our attention on realizing *what* we and all things truly and ultimately are. The answer to that question, profoundly experienced and brilliantly articulated, is that the "what" of our existence is Nothingness.

If this is correct, and I find it convincing, the Christian God is *not* the answer to the Buddhist question, and the Buddhist Nirvana is *not* the answer to the Christian questions. This leaves open the possibility that the Christian God *is* the answer to the Christian questions and that the Buddhist Nirvana *is* the answer to the Buddhist question. Since Christians have at times asked also the Buddhist question, we clearly have much to learn from the Buddhists. For the present we will leave aside the question whether they can also learn from us.

This does not mean that with this clarification of the relation of Buddhism and Christianity we can simply return to our habitual ways of thinking about God. In the first place I have already made clear that I believe the encounter has done us a great service in forcing us to unscramble the confused elements in our thought of God as that has been shaped by our tradition. It drives us back to recover aspects of the biblical faith which even the Reformation return to Scripture missed. It forces us to give up the self-destructive notion of omnipotence that has plagued so much of Christian theology, Catholic and Protestant, to our own day, and to attend once again to the kind of power attributed to God in Scripture generally and in the Genesis account of creation in particular. And on the basis of this it requires that we rethink the mode of God's relation to the world.

How then should we think of God's agency in bringing the world out of chaos into a good order? First it is striking that God does this by speaking. If we were asked, in ignorance of Scripture, how we might image a powerful (and anthropomorphic) God making our world out of chaos, I suspect that most of us would introduce God's hands as the agency. We do occasionally find in Scripture the image of potter and clay (Isaiah 45:9–11 and Romans 9:20–21). But in the crucial accounts, both in Genesis and in John's prologue, the agency of creation is the word. Further, the word of God is not an entity other than God, an intermediary between God and the world. The word, without ceasing to be God's word, is also that which informs the world, that which gives form to the chaos. In John's account it is the light that enlightens every person and the life of all that lives.

If we ask, now, whether God is the efficient cause of the world, the answer is surely affirmative. The primordial chaos is not a world, and it is God's agency alone that creates the world. Further, this agency is not the final causality of Aristotle's unmoved mover but the agency of a God who acts and reacts. But this affirmative answer, so consistently given in the Christian tradition, is easily, even usually, misunderstood. For example, in much of the tradition it has been held that the efficient cause is external to the effect while containing it. That means that God contains the world while remaining external to the world. Here again we meet the omnipotent God who has nothing with which to interact, and we have a world from which God is absent, a world that can lead the mind to God only by modes of reasoning that have been exposed today as unsound. No. The efficient causality exercised by God in the creation of the world, according to our scriptural sources, is much more like that described in the first lecture. It is the effect that contains the cause. The word, the light, and the life communicated by God to the world are constitutive of the world as God's actual presence in the world. They give form to the world, but in doing so they bring into being a world that can thwart as well as fulfill God's purposes. This is so because what is imparted by God to the world is not its matter. That matter in itself has no agency over against God, but as it is formed by God it contributes a measure of autonomy to the agency of what is formed.

The first response to the Buddhist challenge is thus to purify our Christian thought of God from all suggestion that God is the whatness of whatever is. That whatness is Nirvana, and we will do well to recognize in Nirvana a more profound grasp of the chaos of the biblical account. We can learn not to think pejoratively of chaos, but, after the Oriental fashion, to respect it and appreciate it. It is the nature of Being as such.

But the Buddhist has given us clearer images of Nothingness than those I have suggested thus far. Of these the most important and most fully developed is *Sunyata* or Emptiness. Nothingness is not the sheer absence of something, it is perfect receptivity and openness. This is clarified further in the idea of *pratitya-samutpada* or dependent origination. According to this mode of explanation, whatever-is is a momentary conjunction of all that it is not. That is, each event or occurrence is constituted by its reception of all the forces that impinge upon it. Entities do not first exist and then receive from others. The entity is nothing but this reception. It is an evanescent coalescence of the world. *What* a thing is, then, is receptive emptiness, nothing more. And since such Emptiness is characterized precisely by lacking any character or form or substance of its own, it is Nothingness.

Now this poses a more serious challenge to Christian thought of God. We must understand that the Buddhist is realizing and explaining the ultimate reality of whatever is. There can be no exceptions. The total and unqualified interrelatedness of all things is such that there cannot be, alongside what is Empty, some other entity that has substantial existence. The Buddhist imagination can populate the universe with Buddhas who function very much as gods, and it can even speak of gods in distinction from Buddhas, but these Buddhas and any deities there are must be Empty, that is, their true nature, like the nature of all things, is Emptiness.

In discussions between Christians and Buddhists this has often been the most troublesome point. Even when Christians avoid thinking of God as the substantial Being of all things, they still attribute to God what the Buddhist can only hear as substantial characteristics. And it may be that no doctrine of God can ever be formulated that answers the Christian questions without violating the Buddhist sensibility.

This chapter is not the place to pursue in metaphysical detail the possibility of satisfying the Buddhist requirement. Our question is instead what we as Christians can learn of God in this encounter. And the answer here is that we can listen to the Buddhist to hear what is existentially offensive in the idea of substance, why a God conceived to be substantial must be experienced by the Buddhist as inferior. The Christian must believe that God is "perfect" in some sense. Hence, it is important to formulate our ideas of perfection with as much sensitivity as possible. We can hone that sensitivity in relation to the Buddhist who declares perfect only the completely Empty One, or perhaps better, only those who realize their complete Emptiness.

It is not hard for Christians to grasp some of what is meant here. We, too, speak of emptying ourselves of our self-centeredness, our pride, our desires for fame and wealth, our prejudices, our defensiveness, and so forth. In prayer we may seek to empty our minds of all our cares and hopes so as to be more open to God. We can see in the Buddhist disciplines more sustained and systematic programs

of self-emptying than any we have attempted. There remains a difference in that we empty ourselves so as to be receptive primarily
to God, whereas the Buddhist regards this direction of attention as
a limitation upon emptiness that must also be overcome. But at least
we can appreciate in general, if vaguely, the reason for seeking
Emptiness.

Among the mystics some have also spoken of the divine Emptiness, and this has not always meant that, with Eckhart, they have
turned from God to Godhead. No, they have experienced God as
also Empty. In the New Testament we read of the famous *kenosis*
or self-emptying whereby the Son of God became a human being
(Philippians 2:6–8). Thus the themes of divine self-emptying and of
divine Emptiness are not wholly strange to our tradition. Still they
are a minor note in the whole.

What would it mean to think of God's emptiness in a way stimulated by the encounter with Buddhism? It would mean that the divine reality was constituted by perfect openness to, and reception
of, whatever is possible as possible and whatever is actual as actual.
It would mean that there were no divine purposes or attitudes or
interests that interfered with such perfect receptivity. It would mean
that the response to what was received was perfectly appropriate to
what was received rather than being distorted by any antecedent
purpose or intention.

Such a vision would not exclude God's efficacy in the world. On
the contrary, the Buddhist vision of *pratitya-samutpada* ensures that
every event would receive God as part of its own constitution, just
as God would receive every event into the divine life.

This is not the way that Christians have usually thought of God.
The language is very different from that of the Bible. Yet if we reflect on the meaning of perfect love it can lead us in this direction.
Are not lovers, ideally, fully open to those they love, responding
appropriately to their present feelings rather than operating on prior
agenda? Do not lovers offer themselves to those they love to be
experienced in turn for what they are without imposing alien aims
and purposes upon the beloved? Perhaps through our encounter
with the Buddhist ideal of Emptiness we can purify our thought of
God's love from inappropriate elements of judgment and favoritism
and coercion.

There is a final mystery for the Christian believer in God raised by the encounter with Buddhism. We have thought that all the good in the world is made possible by God and that the greatest goods, especially the supreme spiritual gifts, arise as people attend to God and trust God. We have felt that the denial of God, while not preventing God from working, nevertheless ran counter to the highest religious experiences of peace and joy. Yet in Buddhism we see saints who fully match our own who understand their attainment as dependent in part upon their total denial of God. We seem to be driven either to deny this historical evidence or else to attribute to God a peculiar effectiveness among some of those who deny or ignore God's existence. Of these the latter is far the more Christian option.

But how can we affirm God's peculiar efficacy among those who deny God's reality? The answer must come from further consideration of what occurs in the achievement of Emptiness. When we are not Empty, or when we have not realized our Emptiness, we undertake to direct our own attention and receptiveness according to our beliefs. Our beliefs are shaped by many factors, and even if some of them approach accuracy, they never conform perfectly to the world. We have already seen in these lectures the extent to which our ways of thinking about God have been confused and erroneous. Hence even when we attempt to attend to God, to trust God, and to listen to God's Word, that to which we direct our attention is not in fact God as God really is. Our beliefs are a screen between us and God. Further, our effort to listen to God is never free from a mixture of motives. There are some things we would prefer not to hear from God. And this fear that God may not say what we want to hear clouds our listening. In this way belief in God and attention to the God in whom we believe is bound up with concepts, preferences, hopes, and fears. It is, in the Buddhist sense, a form of clinging.

The Buddhist rejects belief in God not primarily for theoretical reasons, but because it is a form of clinging. To become Empty is to be free from such clinging. But this does not mean that the realization of Emptiness is being cut off from the rest of reality in a self-enclosed moment. On the contrary, to be Empty is to be filled by all that is without prejudice or distortion. If, as we Christians believe, all-that-is includes God, then God is part of that which fills the Empty One.

Furthermore, when one is Empty, each aspect of what-is plays that role in filling one that is appropriate to its own nature. What is appropriate to God is the giving of freedom together with that direction of self-constitution which is best in that situation. Hence the Empty One, precisely by being free from all self-direction, is directed by God. From the Christian perspective this explains why the realization of a state described as beyond all moral differentiations of better and worse, right and wrong, consistently expresses itself in ways that appear good and right.

The purpose of this chapter has been to confront Christian theism with the reality, power, and beauty of a great traditional Way that has rejected theism. This confrontation forces us to ask whether Christians can continue to believe in God when we see that precisely through withdrawing attention from God Buddhists achieve saintliness. My answer thus far has been that from our point of view the Buddhist achievement can be interpreted theistically. But the challenge goes deeper. If precisely the rejection of such interpretations has facilitated the Buddhist achievement, is it not perverse to insist on retaining it—even if we can do so with conceptual consistency?

The answer can only be that from the Christian point of view there are some important attainments that have been advanced by attention to features of reality from which Buddhists withdraw interest. For example, in the first lecture I talked about science. Science develops only where there is intense interest in and sustained attention to forms. Buddhism has discouraged that, whereas Christian theism over a period of many centuries nurtured it. Similarly Christian theism has encouraged attention to questions of justice in social organization in ways that the Buddhist ideal of Emptiness has not.

This might suggest that we Christians should retain an overarching theism while adopting for religious purposes a non-theistic stance. Such a proposal has at least the virtue of reversing an unhealthy trend in the modern West toward relegating God to a narrowly religious and personal sphere! But to exclude attention to God from the religious and personal sphere would also be a major abridgment of Christian theism. Christians such as Thomas Merton and William Johnston have worked sensitively and critically to learn from Buddhism in such a way as to inform and transform inherited practices of theistic devotion. Perhaps in time faith in God can be so freed from its association with clinging that Christians can risk losing what they have known as God for the sake of being conformed to God.

CHAPTER SIX

God and Feminism

by John B. Cobb

I n my first chapter I asked whether belief in God is compatible with being fully informed by the scientific spirit and by what science has shown us about our world. I argued that indeed it is if we cease to think of God as the one cause of all things or the sole cause of any event or entity and think of God instead as the giver of life and freedom, the source of creative novelty, the one who in love creates the possibility of our love. I have claimed that to adjust our thinking about God in this way is not to retreat from larger claims that once more fully expressed the logic of faith. Instead, this way of thinking of God states more clearly what faith has intended. The encounter with science compels us from without to purify our thought of God from views of power that are sub-Christian. In this sense, at least, science is a resource for thinking about God.

In my second chapter I described the challenge that comes to belief in God from the discovery in the East that beliefs in deities, more or less resembling Christian theism, belong to the less developed stages of the religious life. Especially in major forms of Buddhism every belief in God is seen as a form of clinging that blocks our achievement of the ultimate goal—Nirvana. Here is a challenge to Christian belief in God from within the area of religious experience itself. I have responded by showing that there is no necessary contradiction between belief in God and Buddhist assertions about the reality, when the nature of God is rethought in light of Buddhist criticisms. I have argued that the removal from our image of God of every element of substantiality is a gain in the purity of our expression of what is known in faith, and that in this sense Buddhism, too, is a resource for our thinking about God. The practical question that remains as yet unsettled is whether the Christian can existentially experience Buddhist Emptiness without relinquishing faith in God.

The encounter with the contemporary women's movement raises quite different questions about God. Whereas many in our time have come to the conclusion that the thought of God has lost its power, feminist theologians have shown us once again that the idea of God is bound up with the deepest attitudes of life. These inherited attitudes shape the behavior of both women and men—often quite unconsciously—and for the most part they function to restrict and oppress women.

If the Christian God is part of the fabric and sanction of an oppressive system, feminists ask, can women really continue to worship "Him"? Indeed, if the worship of God supports and reinforces this system, must women seeking liberation from this system not oppose all worship of God? Alternatively, can our ideas and experience of God be so altered that worship of God will become part of the liberation of women instead of their continued oppression?

There are special problems involved when a male theologian addresses questions of this sort, problems of such seriousness that it often seems that silence is the only appropriate role. Women are rightly reacting against millennia-long conditions in which men have undertaken to speak for women and to determine the structure of relationships between women and men. Women properly assert that they should speak for themselves and that men should listen.

But to listen seriously to what women are saying is to be affected in one's total perspective and understanding. For a male theologian to listen seriously is to have his received ways of thinking of God placed in a quite new light, a light that reveals their inadequacy and falseness. Such an experience requires a theological response involving changes in language and conceptuality and in the understanding of the church and the theological enterprise.

I would like, accordingly, to make clear that in this chapter I am not trying to give advice and counsel to the women's movement or to feminist theologians. I think I understand how inappropriate and unwelcome such an effort would be. On the other hand, I am not trying to expound and support their views. They are far better able to do that themselves. Instead, I shall indicate what fresh reflection about God has been stimulated in me as a male theologian by my encounter with the women's movement.

There is a second difficulty in undertaking this topic. Whereas science and Buddhism have been around for a long time, the current women's movement is very young. Some generalizations about science and Buddhism can be formulated on the basis of a large, established literature. This is not possible with respect to feminism. As women break through to creative freedom they move rapidly from height to height and from depth to depth. The cutting edge of their insights and concerns in one year is overtaken in the next. This dynamism is a mark of vitality. It reinforces the feminist sense that only from inside the movement can it be understood and interpreted. A male listener can at best respond to particular ideas generated by the movement from time to time, recognizing that these are abstracted from the dynamic flow. This chapter would be more accurately entitled: "God and Some Challenges to Christian Theism Suggested to a Male Theologian by the Women's Movement."

That title seems clumsy, but I hope that I have made clear, first that this chapter is not about feminism and, second, that it certainly does not pretend to be presented from the feminist point of view. It is a male theologian's response to a simple but extremely important charge that he has heard as he has listened to feminists. This charge is that males have worshipped a male deity and foisted this worship of maleness on females as well.

When first confronted with this charge we men are likely to respond defensively that it is ridiculous. We insist that we have always known that God as Spirit is beyond gender. The whole question of gender suggests an anthropomorphism that we believe ourselves to have outgrown. True, we speak of God as "he," but that, we think, is only because of long-established conventions, first, that when both sexes are involved the masculine gender is used inclusively, and, second, that when the gender is indeterminate, but the personal character is important, we use the masculine gender neutrally.

However, this whole convention is now under sharp and critical attack. We have been made conscious of the fact that when we refer "neutrally" to a person as "he" we have in fact favored both in our own minds and in the minds of the hearers the image of a male. That the "he" would be a female is felt as the exception. Where the roles we have in mind are predominantly occupied by women, as with secretaries or nurses, for example, we shift to "she" when we have no other knowledge of the situation. In other words, the neutral use of "he" is not so neutral after all.

The insistence by women that we avoid the supposedly neutral "he" in referring to persons seems to many people to be too small a matter to warrant the attention it receives. However, it has a practical and existential importance that is far greater than initially appears. Human beings are linguistic creatures, and a change of language is a change of consciousness. To change one's habits of speech, many of us can testify, is also a consciousness-raising event. It forces us to examine the images associated with the words and the habits of mind and attitudes associated with these images. Perhaps eventually we will be able to arrive at a neutral singular pronoun, but meanwhile we must learn to live with the awkwardness of its lack.

If the use of the masculine for neutral purposes has led to serious distortion in reference to humans, we must look again at our language about God. Has it not, despite our protestations, carried with it the image of God as male? Do we not think of God, the Father, as loving us as a father does rather than as a mother does? Do we not find it shocking, even threatening, to hear God referred to as "she"? Does this not tell us men that, despite our protestations, we do in fact worship a male God? Does this not mean that we have deified maleness? Is this not idolatry? Are we not guilty as charged?

When we men recognize our guilt, we may try first to unburden ourselves by what we call "cleaning up our sexist language." If our intention all along has not been sexist, as we like to think, and if we discover that nevertheless the sexist language has led to sexist images, we are required for the sake of our own liberation to find a language that is free from the insidious male bias.

There are several ways to do this. One is simply to repeat the word God and to avoid the use of the pronoun. I have employed this device in these chapters. Another is to use the neuter pronoun with "deity" instead of "God," as the antecedent. These shifts in linguistic usage can be made without seriously jarring the hearer.

A more radical proposal is to use "he or she" with respect to God as we are learning to do with respect to persons neutrally referred to. It is also possible to alternate the use of the pronouns. One proposal is to identify the third person of the Trinity as feminine and hence refer to the Holy Spirit as she, while allowing the Father and the Son to be he

The chief value of such experiments is to raise our consciousness about the extent to which our images of God have been male. As this happens we can consciously introduce more female images into our thinking about God. Eventually the use and power of female images may remove the still-jarring effect of referring to God as she.

For the present, however, it is important for us to recognize and reflect upon the shocking fact that the God we have worshiped really has been masculine. This is not a metaphysical statement, but it is a statement about metaphysical thinking about God as much as about religious images. Historically, whatever God's true nature and identity may be, God has been experienced, conceived, and spoken of as masculine.

The masculine character of God has not always been viewed as a minor matter. The history of religion knows female as well as male Gods. In the religious imagination of antiquity the sexual character of the Gods was far from muted. There was no doubt in the Hebrew mind that Yahweh was a male God. The use of the masculine pronoun and of masculine images was certainly not incidental.

Nevertheless, the Hebrews in considerable measure desexualized Yahweh. Indeed, one reason for the choice by men of a male deity over a female deity was that only in relation to the male could men partly desexualize their experience of the divine. Men could relate to a male as a person without regard to specifically sexual attributes; but not to a female. Yahweh was denied a consort, and any thought of Yahweh as involved in sexual activity was wholly blasphemous. In other words, in order to envision God as transcendent of sexual involvement and interests, God had to be conceived by males as male.

This development in Israel is paralleled by that in Greece. The Greek philosophers were well acquainted with a pantheon of male and female deities. They found the stories of the antics of these gods disgusting. For them the thought of deity was of a reality radically transcendent of such matters. So they affirmed one God, which they too conceived, although less anthropomorphically than the Hebrews, as masculine.

Similar developments took place in the emergence of the higher religions in the East. The movement from polytheism to different forms of monism or the quest for a principle that transcended the multiplicity of the world was associated with leaving sexual differentiation behind, but it was through the image of the male that this was done.

The distinction of masculine and feminine in deity has deep roots. Typically the deities of earth and soil are female, the deities of the sky, male. To this day this imagery has a deep hold upon us. The God who is up there and out there seems male; but when we turn to the God of the depths, female imagery pours in upon us. As women have made us keenly aware, there is a close connection in our male imagination between the body, the earth, and the female, over all of which we men experience ourselves as transcendent lords, sharing this transcendence, perhaps, with the purely transcendent one, God.

Given this history of the male imagination, it is no light matter to introduce feminine language and feminine images into our thought of God. Images are too deep and too powerful to be readily exorcised, and our religious life is richly informed—consciously and unconsciously—by these images. The religious life that is oriented to a female deity is different from that oriented to a male deity. We need to ask ourselves whether this is a shift we can affirm, or whether, indeed, we can affirm even a partial movement in this direction.

Let me reemphasize that I am here reflecting as a man about the meaning of the new sexual consciousness for men. I am not saying that for women the male God is more transcendent of sexuality than the female God. That is a difficult question, since the male has exercised dominant influence on public images and their written transmission. What we know of the female gods is chiefly what they meant to men, not what they meant to women. The historical interest of women, therefore, centers more upon the rediscovery of the understanding of deity in matriarchal cultures, that is, in cultures where women rather than men shaped the public images. For some women, it is possible to idealize those cultures and envision the hoped-for future as in some measure a return to them. From such hopes men are excluded.

On the other hand, men can discover attractive elements in the earlier religious forms that gave prominence, if not dominance, to female deities. The tension between men's sexuality and their spirituality was far less in that context. Every aspect of their being was recognized and given its due in relation to some deity, whereas with the rise of the one transcendent God a hierarchical order was imposed on the inner life. Nevertheless, the achievement of responsible, personal existence with its partial transcendence of the bodily and emotional life is one that is not lightly to be cast aside. Indeed, one of the complaints of women is that they have been too much excluded from the attainment of such transcendent personhood.

My own conviction is that we must view our history dialectically. We may suppose a prehistorical matriarchal culture in which hierarchical structures and role definitions were less oppressive. We may suppose that in that culture there was little internalized guilt and anxiety, a strong feeling of mutual belonging and participation, and little inhibition of the expression of feeling and desire. The emergence of male dominance shattered this harmony. What it achieved was a new kind of personhood. In this it was aided by the transformation of religious images and the heightening of the divine transcendence. But for the attainment of male liberation a price was exacted from the female.

Indeed, this price has been enormous. Women have been exploited, enslaved, dehumanized, and objectified. This factual debasement has been rationalized by a vilification that has been sanctioned by the highest authorities including the Christian church. Women have been forced to serve men's sexual purposes by men who have felt shame in their own sexuality and have dealt with their shame by projecting it on women.

The demand that women be subservient was a need of the male not because of his full liberation but because of its limited and precarious character. The male who is confident in his inner strength as a whole person has nothing to fear from the liberation of the female. But the male who cannot incorporate his sexuality into his liberated personhood requires for his sexual potency and enjoyment a subordinated female.

The time is now long overdue for a new movement of the dialectic. Women cannot wait for men so to complete their liberation that

they are fully ready for the liberation of women as well. We have
had our chance. Our liberation has gone far enough that women
have been able to taste some of the elements of liberation. That
taste is sufficient to whet the appetite for more. So women are demanding full liberation, believing that only as they liberate themselves will the liberation of men also be completed.

This can be translated simply into full equality of men and women
with optimal opportunities for both to develop their personhood.
But this is not the full message of the women's movement. In their
taste of what men have achieved in terms of liberation into responsible personhood, they have also sensed its limitations more clearly
than have men. Men have been calling for wholeness, but women
do so with keener existential passion and insight. They do not want
to swap the partial wholeness they have known for the tensions and
anxieties of transcendence. They want wholeness and transcendence.

Men can view this cry as naive and utopian. We, too, would like
to have both wholeness and transcendence, but we have learned
through painful experience that they are in tension with one another. For the most part we have settled for transcendence without
wholeness. But alternatively, with greater faith, we may credit the
women's vision. Perhaps personal wholeness with transcendence has
been impossible thus far because transcendence has been connected with the oppression of women. Perhaps if men and women
seek it together, under the guidance of liberated women, the longed-
for wholeness can be renewed without the sacrifice of transcendence.

This would complete the dialectical process. We begin with the
thesis of wholeness in a matriarchal society. We set against that the
antithesis of the liberation of males in a patriarchal society. We now
seek a synthesis in the liberation of females without loss of wholeness. Since in this final stage the leadership must be in the hands of
women, we may think of it as a new matriarchy, although this need
not mean the hierarchical social subordination of men.

To interpret what is now occurring as the culmination of a vast
historical dialectic may be an exaggeration. The present women's
movement may be no more than a minor ripple leaving behind
greater equality under the law but no profound change in our exis-

tence. Even if that should prove true, I suggest that the historical situation is such that this ripple will be followed by larger waves until eventually a more fundamental existential revolution is accomplished.

History is full of ironies. In the name of peace we fight wars; in the name of Christ we torture; and in the name of liberty we enslave. The present stage of the women's movement is no exception. Its mission is to bring wholeness with transcendence. Its effect is to introduce new tensions, anxieties, and guilt. The rhetoric of the movement is confused and its leaders are divided. Nevertheless, even now men can learn much from what is occurring as the leadership in working out the relations between the sexes passes back, after these millennia, into the hands of women. Our response as males may determine whether in fact we are witnessing the birth pangs of a great historical synthesis or only a new abortive struggle that will leave unhealed wounds.

My topic here is the response of a male theologian to the feminist unveiling of the maleness of our traditional God. I have set this topic in the context of a vast historical dialectic, for otherwise it tends to seem abstract, and women have taught us that our images of deity are intimately bound up with our total existence. Men must now acknowledge that our worship has been distorted by our own need for liberation in such a way as to inhibit the liberation of women. We can also see that our liberation is forever incomplete as long as it is based on the oppression of women and the exclusion of the feminine from that which we worship. Accordingly, while we listen to those women who are struggling to recast their faith in ways appropriate to their new insights, we must continue our own work of rethinking God.

If my previous comments have merit, then the deeper question is that of the relation of transcendence and wholeness. The vision of a radically transcendent God accompanied the movement toward transcendence for men. But the loss of human wholeness on the part of men was associated with images of God that also lacked this wholeness. This is expressed in one-sidedly masculine characterizations of the one transcendent God.

The one-sidedly masculine transcendent God appeared in fullest form in the Newtonian age. Newton's deistic God stands radically outside his creation. (I say "his" advisedly in this case, for it is clear that this God is a modern male sky God.) This God commands and demands and justly rewards and justly punishes the actions of his creatures.

Rooted in the mystical tradition of Jacob Boehme and Friedrich Schelling, Paul Tillich has provided us with an alternative way of thinking of God. Tillich's more pantheistic God is the being of all things in so far as being is understood in its unitary depths. (This is the metaphysical version of the Mother Gods of the Earth.) To exist is to rise out of these depths only to be drawn back into them again. Tillich's God contains and grounds our being even in our assertion of our individuality in freedom, but that assertion is somehow also a necessary estrangement from God. We are called to have the courage to be despite the pain of this estrangement, but it is not clear how that call can come from God. It seems more the male struggle for liberation from the all-embracing and all-consuming Mother.

I am suggesting that although Tillich provides us with a God we might characterize as feminine, this is "feminine" from the traditional perspective of the male. Hence the move from the Newtonian Father to the Tillichian Mother would not in itself suffice to support the full liberation of both sexes. The worship of this God might confirm the sense of wholeness in the depths but not encourage the always partly rebellious assertion of transcendence.

If we have in Newton's God transcendence without wholeness and in Tillich's God wholeness without transcendence, we need an understanding of God as inclusive of both. We need to think of God as the prod and the lure to liberation and transcendence, and at the same time the inclusive wholeness to which that transcendence distinctively contributes.

In the two preceding chapters I sketched elements of a doctrine of God as these are suggested in response to the challenges of the scientific worldview and of Buddhism. In the first, the emphasis was on God as the source of relevant possibilities through which we are empowered to transcend the past and constitute ourselves by our own free decisions. In the second, the emphasis was on the "Emptiness" of God in the sense that God has no substance or character except openness to all that is. This openness is Emptiness, and this Emptiness is perfect fullness. It is appropriate now to test these ideas against the new challenge offered by feminist theology. Can the worship of God in this sense be appropriately liberating for women? Can it assist their guidance of men into the new wholeness that lies beyond transcendence?

To me it seems that this is a hopeful direction to pursue. In this vision, the God who calls and goads us toward freedom and transcendence is also the God who responds tenderly to our failures as well as to our successes and who achieves in her own life a harmonious unity of all that is. Here I have risked the feminine pronoun out of the conviction that as we reflect upon this aspect of deity, its responsive, tender, and inclusive wholeness, the feminine motif asserts itself in our male imagination. But this is a feminine from which the male does not need to become free through courageous self-assertion. On the contrary, this is a feminine whose reality reassures us that, as we take the risk of freedom, whatever happens, we are loved and that taking the risk is in itself important.

Mary Daly has charged that even if the idea of God were so changed as to escape its offensively masculine character, Christianity would remain a male religion. This is because God is seen in history in the form of a male, the man Jesus. Whatever God may be apart from our history, God is mediated to us in masculine form. For the liberated woman, she insists, this is unacceptable.

There can be little doubt that Christianity has been and now is a male-dominated religion. Male domination is characteristic of all the major religious Ways. All were founded by men, all have been governed by men, and the public shaping of their basic images has been dominated by men. It is arguable as to which among them have done better, and which worse, by women. A case can be made that Jesus himself was remarkably free from typical attitudes of men toward women, but this is scant comfort for women who find that these typical attitudes have governed the church to our own time. Further, the fact that Jesus was a man and chose men as his key disciples is still used at times as an argument against the ordination of women. Hence there is no gainsaying Mary Daly's point that Christianity is a religion founded by a man and controlled by men, within which women's contributions have been carefully restricted and contained.

If we are now to argue that although this has been true in the past, Christianity need not remain a male-oriented faith, we are saying something very significant and even radical. Mary Daly is saying that male-orientation is of the essence of Christianity. If Christianity has an essence, it is difficult to deny that a part of that essence is the worship of God through the male, Jesus Christ, the one mediator between God and the world. Other elements in the church's thought and practice have not balanced this male-orientation. Hence to say that Christianity need not continue to be male-oriented in this way is to deny that it can be understood in terms of an essence. It is to assert that Christianity is a living movement that can become what it has not been. What seems essential to its being in one period may become peripheral in another and may even disappear in a third.

I am not suggesting, however, that in our day Jesus has become peripheral to the most vital elements in the Christian movement, much less that he has disappeared. I am suggesting that the way we understand his role has changed and can change, and that the further changes that are required if Christianity is to become a truly liberating movement for all of us are possible.

Jesus did not come to proclaim himself or even to proclaim the reality of God. Jesus understood his mission as the preaching of the Kingdom of God. He directed his followers not to himself but to that which he heralded. His own importance lay in his announcement of the kingdom and in his preparation of those who responded. Through their response, the kingdom was already fragmentarily realized in his own table fellowship and ministry, but it was still to the coming kingdom that Jesus directed attention.

In the words of Bultmann, after the resurrection of Jesus, the proclaimer became the proclaimed. The church directed attention to the Jesus who had proclaimed the kingdom and was vindicated in his resurrection rather than to the kingdom he proclaimed. That kingdom the church identified partly with its own life and partly with eschatological judgment. At times Christian communities undertook to realize the kingdom on earth at least in anticipatory forms, and the eschatological element has never been entirely lost, but for the most part the church became Christocentric.

In recent theology something of the balance present in Jesus' own understanding has been recovered. In Catholic circles Teilhard de

Chardin turned attention to the future consummation as the meaning-giving focus of all our interests. He saw Jesus as playing an initiatory role in the process of Christogenesis through which the Omega is being formed. Omega is an inclusive wholeness of all in which personal transcendence is not lost but fulfilled. Wolfhart Pannenberg has similarly renewed in Protestant circles the focus on the coming Kingdom which is the resurrection of the dead. Jesus' importance is as proclaimer of that Kingdom whose message was vindicated by the proleptic occurrence of that Kingdom in his own resurrection. For him, too, the Kingdom is a unity or wholeness in which personal transcendence is fulfilled.

As a modern Christian, I question how literally I can or should take the expectation of an actual consummation of the historical process. It seems possible that history may end in self-extinction rather than in consummation. But I am convinced that we should be guided by images of hope that arise out of our faith through serious confrontation with the problems and possibilities of our time. The Christian's attention should not be on what has happened but on what will or can happen. Of course, her or his perceptions are shaped by the past and are sharpened by repeated return to their sources of nourishment. But our judgments about how to order the life of the church and society should not be derived from how this was done in the first century. They should be derived instead from our anticipation of how they will be ordered in whatever we can understand to be the hoped for and fulfilling future, that which counts for us as the Kingdom of God.

It is true that the phrase "Kingdom of God" is masculine. But we are certainly not bound to that. Kingdom translates *basileia*, which in the Greek is feminine, as is the corresponding word in Hebrew. It is true also that the image of the Kingdom is associated with ideas of hierarchical authority and judgment in ways that may also be decried as masculine. But on the whole, Christian visions of the future fulfillment are less skewed in a masculine direction than are other features of Christian thought. In the End, it is recognized, there will no longer be discrimination between male and female. The wholeness that is envisaged includes both.

It would make an interesting study to examine Christian eschatology from the feminist perspective. I assume that, in addition to some fruitful images, much would be found that would prove offensive. But this is not what is important to me now. Our present visions of the fulfilled or consummated future will be informed by our new awareness of the rightful claims of women. Indeed it is they who are most convincingly envisioning a new future that will break from the past while growing out of it. They are even now trying to live toward and out of that future. It will be a future in which the masculine is subsumed within a new feminine.

Christianity as a movement will not be faithless to Jesus in following the leadership of women in the envisaging of a new future. On the contrary, it will be a more appropriate response to his call to live toward and out of the *basileia* than has been most of the Christianity in the intervening years. As the vision grows and changes, so the Christian movement will adjust and adapt. It cannot know in advance what aspects of its past will prove indispensable resources and what will prove to be the false riches that cannot be carried into the new age. Christianity must find its way in response to the continuing work of divine liberation.

In my own view there should be conformation between the End as we envisage it before us in our history and the inclusive wholeness that is the everlasting life of God. In this sense our prayer must be that God's will be done on earth as it is in Heaven. This means that as in God we can distinguish between the giver of freedom, who urges us to dare great things, and the assuring lover, who accepts us in both success and failure, so in history we can distinguish between Jesus, who calls us to live from the New Age, and the New Age toward which he directs us. In our view of God we can see that the two sides call forth imagery that is respectively masculine and feminine, but that it is finally the feminine that includes the masculine. So in history we can see that the male Jesus is finally taken up into a unity which we can learn to experience as a new form of the feminine.

The time has now come to bring this chapter, and this section of the book, to a conclusion. There are many loose ends. In fact, I am leaving you mostly with loose ends.

Nevertheless, my intention has been that these chapters be suggestive of a hopeful and exciting situation in regard to our conceiving of God. What has seemed distressing has been that the in-

herited doctrine is attacked in so many ways from so many conflict-
ing sources. In that situation it seemed there could not be enough
hands to stop the leaks in the dike. It seemed only a matter of time
before the possibility of belief in God would be gone for thoughtful,
openminded people. That has been an increasingly widespread feeling in our time, and many have acted upon it by simply giving up
the belief. But if it turns out that the fresh reflection we do in response to one critique leads to ways of conceiving of God that are
appropriate to the response to other critiques as well, then it may
be that a new understanding of God is emerging that can have widespread relevance and convincing power. If such conceiving of God
can inspire people to creative imagination and personal dedication
intelligently directed, if it can draw us into a deeper understanding
of people of other traditions, if it can heal the divisions that arise in
our own corporate life as Christians, then the death of God may
indeed be followed by the resurrection of God.

I have certainly proved nothing so grandiose in these chapters.
Each would require vast development, and the whole would need
to be tested in relation to other topics of equal importance to those
that have been treated. Three such topics come particularly to mind.

One is the problem of evil. The faith in God of numerous persons,
simple and scholarly, has foundered in confrontation with the horrors of history or with personal suffering. They ask, how can a good
God cause or allow such appalling evils. And the answers they have
heard from traditional theists and popular pietists have been profoundly unsatisfactory. It is my conviction, however, that there is
an answer, and that the kind of thinking about God that I have proposed in these lectures embodies it. It requires that we transform
our notions of God's power. God's power is the power that makes
us free. It is incompatible with the sort of power that would inter-
fere with the consequences of our actions. At each moment God
creates new freedom in the world we have made by the way we
have used our past freedom. Since I cannot say more about this
here, I would like to call attention to a recent book by David Griffin,
God, Power, and Evil, in which he lucidly and painstakingly shows
the failure of classical theism to respond to this burning question
and provides an answer that is in harmony with the way of conceiving of God that I have offered.

A second topic is the environmental crisis as it has heightened our awareness of our disastrous attitudes and relations to the creatures with whom we share this planet. Again, traditional forms of Christianity have been part of the problem more than part of the solution, and even now they continue to play this role. The traditional doctrine of God has been central to the misdirection of our efforts and attention. To continue to worship God in such a way that our attention is withdrawn from our interconnectedness with the whole creation and is focused only on our own inwardness before him (again, I use the masculine advisedly) will only heighten our destructiveness. It intensifies our sense of the distinctness of the human from the rest of the created world and encourages us to see that world as simply a stage for our human drama. It neglects the extent to which the drama destroys the stage and thus also the possibility of its own continuance. It allows us to try to solve the problems of the poor by ever greater production and thus to avoid the problems of distribution. I have written at length on these matters elsewhere. I mention them here to say that the same adjustments of the concept of God that are called for in the encounter with science, Buddhism, and feminism are needed also in response to the new consciousness of the fragility of the planetary biosphere.

A third topic is political liberation, and here much work remains to be done. There is no doubt that the liberation which Christians are concerned with must be the liberation of oppressed races and classes as well as the giving of freedom to the individual. The God of whom I have been speaking appears individualistic when this contrast is sharply drawn whereas the God of the Old Testament was seen to act in historical events for the sake of the entire people. Advocates of political or liberation theology often stress this contrast and dismiss the kind of theology I have been advocating as bourgeois and pietistic.

In a new way this brings to the fore the old question as to the relation of the individual and the society. Do we change individuals through structural social changes or do we change society through changing individuals? The answer, of course, is that neither can occur effectively except in interaction with the other. A change in consciousness is required before oppressed people will assert their rights, but at the same time, if they do not see a connection between their new consciousness and a changed situation, the new consciousness will remain abstract and ineffective.

The most impressive expression of this indispensable unity with which I am familiar is the work of Paulo Freire. He has developed a "pedogogy of the oppressed" that in the process of teaching oppressed peasants to read also conscienticized them, that is, made them aware of the realities of the situation. This awareness was also empowerment to establish goals and to order action to the achievement of these goals. The teacher trusts the peasants' own wisdom to set goals and to direct action. Thus the teacher functions to break the barrier to the effectiveness of God's liberating work in and through the peasants.

In the form given to political liberation by Freire a bridge can be built between the idea of God developed in these chapters and the more usual images of God that are associated with liberation theology. However, many problems remain. One cannot but wonder whether the effort to adjust the doctrine of God both in relation to the Buddhist realization of Emptiness and in relation to the demands of political theology may be impossible. But it is my hope that it is not. My hope is guided by the faith that there is in reality and truth one God who guides, directs, frees, and empowers us all, individually and collectively. If that is so, we have only to be sufficiently attentive to truth wherever we find it, and the reality of that one God should appear. The adventure of theology is to be about this business.